To Mary... I wish I
had your screened in porch
for a writing spot!
Best wishes,
Linda T

MUSCADINE LINES

A SOUTHERN ANTHOLOGY

Edited By

KATHY HARDY RHODES

Cold Tree Press
Nashville, Tennessee

Library of Congress Control Number: 2006928716

Published by Cold Tree Press
Nashville, Tennessee
www.coldtreepress.com

MUSCADINE LINES

A SOUTHERN ANTHOLOGY

ACKNOWLEDGMENTS

From the Editor:

In memory of my grandparents, *Thomas Tyre Hardy* and *Nora Bernice Neal Hardy*, who taught me all about muscadines and passed down the land where those sweet southern grapes grow wild

In memory of my father, *Wallace Ray Hardy (1/16/1922 – 3/31/2006)*, my link to the aforementioned land and to life.

In honor of *Charlie Rhodes*, my husband, biggest supporter, and technology expert

With thanks to Susie Dunham, Currie Alexander Powers, C. K. Speroff, and Chance Chambers for their skill, talent, and patience during our sessions in a noisy corner of the café in Barnes and Noble, Brentwood, Tennessee, poring over the lines of the fiction herein

With thanks to all the Muscadine writers between these covers, as well as in asouthernjournal.com, for their dedication to the art of writing and their diligence in submitting, editing, and polishing their art. May they be anthologized and savored for years to come!

From the Authors:

In loving memory, we share the joy of this book—creative toil of our minds and pride of our hearts and souls—with those dear to us:

Bill Ashworth—brother-in-law of Julia Lee Pollock

Robert (Bobby) Alvin Blume—son of Nancy Fletcher-Blume

Richard Russell (Dick) Brown—husband of Gilda Griffith Brown

Dr. Michael Grey Colln—son of Louise Colln

L. Turnley Fraker—father of William W. Fraker

Sandy Howd—best friend of Susie Dunham

Lorine Vordenbaum Lockhart—mother of Judy Lockhart DiGregorio

Maureen McCranie—daughter of Lonnye Sue Sims Pearson

Christopher Paul Perutelli—grandson of Marion Bolick Perutelli

Sue Sims—mother of Lonnye Sue Sims Pearson

Jo-Von Tucker—sister of Neil O. Jones

Erika Tweed—lovely lady, encouraging poet, and friend of Jane K. Kretschmann

In memory of those lost in Hurricane Katrina and in honor of the deep, unflagging soul of New Orleans.
—Currie Alexander Powers

FOREWORD

When a writer takes pen in hand to create a story, or sits down at the keyboard to begin a new tale, art is created. Yes, writing is art just as surely as a great painting is art. The artist has a canvas, brush, and palette. A writer has paper or a screen that is his canvas, fingers that are his brush, and a pen or keyboard for his colors. As an idea forms in the writer's mind, it flows through his being and out through his hands. The colors of words swirl about, and magical art is formed.

So with each story we create, we have the potential equivalent of the Pieta. It can be a major work of art or a minor one, but it is still art. Getting this art onto the papers before us compels us to write. We can feel the ideas forming in our minds, and we must capture them before they are hidden from us. We write, we compose, we formulate the stories of our minds.

The artists of words are a community that those who don't have the talent and love of writing can never breach. It is a society that welcomes any race, gender, or age. The *open sesame* key for membership is the ability to create stories or other written forms. And once this membership qualification is verified, one becomes a member of the community for a lifetime.

In this book you will find the art of people who have qualified for the community of writers. In many instances you have their membership applications in these pages. You will be awed by the range of their talent.

As you read these stories, you become a member of another community—the community of appreciative readers. This community is just as important as the community of writers, for without appreciative readers there would be no reason to write. You and I are the yin and the yang, the two dependent sides of a structure that is supported each by the other.

In this book the talents of many stand as the product of one. There are many facets of this book, and there are many pleasures to be found within the pages. Explore all of them. Read the pages with enthusiasm and excitement.

The stories are our gifts to you, the readers. We all live lives that are commonplace in many areas, but in the sunlight of our writing moments we come most alive. These stories are the creations of those sunlit moments. Take them, absorb them, enjoy them, and hopefully, learn from them.

— Jackie K. Cooper, author of
Journey of a Gentle Southern Man,
Chances and Choices, Halfway Home,
and the forthcoming *The Book Binder*

INTRODUCTION

The south has a longstanding tradition of cultivating some of the country's finest writers. In keeping with that custom, *Muscadine Lines: A Southern Anthology* offers you, the reader, the joy of discovering the treasures of promising new voices, as well as seasoned veterans.

Bottled up inside this volume are luscious morsels—the prose and poetry of twenty-eight individual voices. Like muscadines handpicked fresh and fleshy from the vine, then pressed, their juices intricately mingling, filling a vessel, and spilling over their pleasures, so are the voices of *Muscadine Lines*.

This volume is a gathering of stories and poems that epitomize the qualities readers treasure in the best Southern literature—a rich appreciation of language and humor, as well as a dead-on sense of character and place. They evoke themes of hope and love, disappointment and despair, discovery and loss, that are universal in their resonance. The storytellers let their ideas, imaginations, and experiences flow from the vineyards of their minds to the lines on these pages, as they tell of worlds that are fictionally unique, yet realistically akin to our own.

Writers herein have one thing in common: they all submitted works to the e-zine *Muscadine Lines: A Southern Journal*, asouthernjournal.com, during its first year in operation. *Muscadine Lines: A Southern Journal* is a venue for emerging and established writers to publish and/or promote their work on the Internet. A bimonthly online journal, ISSN 1554-8449, it features fiction, essay, memoir, and poetry. In its first year, beginning January 2005, the journal published the works of 70 writers from 20 states, including every state in the Deep South.

Muscadines, *vitis rotundifolia*, are fat purple grapes, thick-skinned musky fruit unique to the South, often bottled into jams, jellies, and wines. Those joyful little morsels about the size of a hog's eye grew abundantly on my grandparents' farm in Mississippi. When I was a little girl, I rode Dixie, the old mare, bareback down a red dirt lane to a vine that grew wild and high. I plucked muscadines right off that vine, popped them into my mouth, and ate them warmed by the August sun. There's nothing sweeter.

Only in the South

Enjoy the fruits of our labor—
fiction, humor, essay, memoir, and more,
Handpicked fresh from the vine.
Pop a morsel in your mouth,
Enjoy the burst of flavor.
Juice—ample, delicious, delightful.
Inhale the sweet grape perfume,
Like fine wine.

Pop the cork and savor the sweetness, the tartness. Let it fill your senses—scribing so rich it will stay with you long after you finish the last line. Enjoy!

— Kathy Hardy Rhodes, Editor

MUSCADINE
LINES

A SOUTHERN ANTHOLOGY

WATCH AND STALK
Kathy Hardy Rhodes

"I watch and stalk," Annie Dillard says in *Pilgrim at Tinker Creek*. She walks about the creekbanks, contemplating the natural world beyond its commonplace surfaces, recording raw details.

If I could write like Annie Dillard, I'd win a Pulitzer Prize. But I don't have her vast surroundings, her sense of wonder and way with words, or her interpretation of those wild, breathtaking moments.

"I wake expectant," she says, "hoping to see a new thing. If I'm lucky I might be jogged awake by a strange bird call. I dress in a hurry, imagining the yard flapping with auks, or flamingos."

My Tinker Creek is a postage stamp with a cedar fence wrapped around it—old pasture trees; new oak, birch, and sycamore; squirrels skittering, burying acorns in pots of mint and thyme; chickadees constructing nests from the dog's shed hair; and a goldfish pond with a waterfall, where mourning doves sip and a black cat dips his paw. A great blue heron once visited here.

"I walk out; I see something," Dillard says, "some event that would otherwise have been utterly missed and lost; or something sees me, some enormous power brushes me with its clean wing, and I resound like a beaten bell."

It's not enough for me, as a writer, to pass through life scratching at the surface. The natural world comes at me in layers, and I peel each one back to see what's there. I train myself to be aware of my surroundings. I study an interesting thing going on. I let my senses run rampant. I discipline myself to be still, empty, to block anything that would impede full interaction with the object of my attention. I consume it, as it consumes me. Then I dramatize the intimate details by laying them out in a line of words across the page, resounding to the rhythm of that beaten bell.

My breakfast table in the bay window is the gateway. I sit and partake. I watch and stalk. Last Saturday morning, it was a bird that staged a coup and captured my day.

I slid a knife inside the steaming oatmeal muffin, spread a glob of butter, and watched it melt. The bay window offered a view of the winter-empty oak, birch, and sycamore. It was about eight.

I spotted something big on the fence above the white barn birdhouse with rusty tin roof and WELCOME sign. It scooted clumsily a few feet down the fencetop to a sunny spot and stopped beside the SEE ROCK CITY birdhouse. I ran to get the camera and binoculars; my husband grabbed an Audubon guide.

"I think it's a hawk," he said.

I flipped to the section on hawks. Sharp-shinned, red-tailed, Cooper's.

I rested the binoculars against my cheekbones and forehead and looked at the bird close up. His front was white, pure, and gleaming in the sun, as though dressed in a Colonial shirt, like gentry. He had some rusty speckled stripes. His back of gray-feathered layers was fluorescent, shiny, like river rocks with water flowing over them, and his long tail had patterned bars of white, black, gray, black, gray, black. He had a flat head, a curved beak, and a mad scowl. His amber eye looked at me.

He was watching me . . . like a hawk. He drew me in, and my ordered day shifted to an engagement between him and me.

He was fixed on the fencetop, a flat rail like a stage. Beneath his feathered trousers, a yellow talon gripped something small. I strained, squinted, and stared, but couldn't tell what it was. He kept a grip, his amber eye on me.

The yard was eerily quiet. Sparrows and chickadees and mourning doves weren't flitting about, settling in birch branches, lingering at feeders. Squirrels weren't trailing tree limbs, racing and chasing each other, hopping from limb to limb to fence to fieldstones around the pond.

About nine thirty the hawk started picking feathers furiously, slinging them to the wind, scattering them. White fluff caught the sun and floated and swirled to the ground. He kept up a pattern of plucking, looking at me, plucking, looking.

I grabbed the binoculars and moved to the couch, rested on my knees, propped my elbows on the back cushions to steady my view, and spied out the window. I was hunched, hiding, stalking. I slunk from window to window to see better.

It was bloody red where the hawk plucked. The predator bit at the body, ripped it apart, gobbled it. A little yellow leg fell to the side. It was a bird. The hawk was having breakfast on my fence.

I'd just eaten three muffins and was witnessing this carnage. My stomach swelled, shrank, swelled again. I shivered, swallowed, and spied some more.

The hawk stopped and rested. At eleven thirty he started again. He bit, nibbled, and glared, then stilled himself. At one thirty he finished his meal. I'd watched his prey dwindle from a black-feathered ball to bloody-red tissue to nothing. He cleaned his beak on the fence, scraped it with his talons, then spread his wings and sailed across the yard and away.

I went to look at his spoils. Dots of red-jellied guts and fluffs of down stuck to the wood on the fencetop. A gizzard lay on a landscaping timber nearby. Feathers were flung about on brown crisps of leaves—long feathers with mockingbird markings.

He got my mockingbird. It was a curious thing, coming to my window every morning, showing up when I mowed grass, always first at the feeder.

A hopeless feeling washed over me. Yesterday, the mockingbird was whole and majestic. Now, he was gone, only a few unwanted traces left.

I watch and stalk, gather and present. My best writing comes from a passion for knowledge, absorbed and reflected. My best writing comes after immersion in my subject, like a river baptism, water washing over me, words flowing from head to paper.

WRITE ABOUT
Joyce A. O. Lee

Words, like anxious messengers,
Spill from my mind,
Creating pictures
Of people I've never known,
Places I've never been,
And events I've never experienced.
I live in two worlds:
The life I'm in,
And the one I've discovered,
And it is endless,
And filled with strange
And bordering people
Come to life
On that blank expectant page.
Peeking at me, taunting.
Fade in, fade out,
Whispering, they say . . .
Write about.

ROY'S CAFÉ PISTACHIO
Julia Lee Pollock

I am sitting at the back table in Roy's Café after church on Sunday, spooning up pistachio salad and listening to conversations. The gossip's always best on Sundays, right after church when people feel freshly cleansed and free of sin, like inhaling Mexican food after a whole week of Slim-Fast.

There is slander in the air today, as I eavesdrop on the two blondes at the table beside me. I lift a forkful of pistachio to my mouth, and I see them look my way and give each other that knowing look, and I hear them whisper something about a car wreck.

Roy's Café is the real deal, with shiny cheap paneling and an old black-and-white tile floor, the kind that was around long before it became trendy. The fried chicken's good today—the breasts are large and tender—and the fried okra is a perfect crunch. The pistachio salad's a nice complement, but it's fluff food—something to keep from filling you up so that you can hold your rolls and finish your cherry cobbler. The tablecloths are plastic red gingham, and over on the jukebox Skeeter Davis is singing "The End of the World."

The blondes pick at their pistachio salad and say something about my sister-in-law, Penny Gibbs, a woman who got away with murder. My brother Sid is in the grave because of her, along with two other husbands and a one-armed Amway salesman.

Sundays are always crowded, and I dine alone in the back corner underneath the hanging basket of plastic ivy. The blondes toy with their fried chicken, then push their plates away and fire up their cigs. They lean forward, face-to-face, gossiping, then pause to tilt their chins upward and to the right as they exhale. They gaze at each other speculatively, as if a part of them suspects their lives will never advance beyond the superficial fluff of their pistachio, and they exude a faint air of disgusted resignation.

At one fifteen I stuff two forks in my purse and slip out behind a family of six without paying. I do this every Sunday, and it brings me great pleasure.

I drive away in my red Jeep Cherokee and go to Mimosa Cemetery where Sid and my parents are buried. It is late July, hot and still. I water the geraniums that sit on either side of the family headstone, as I have every summer Sunday since my parents died. They were killed in a car wreck in 1982 at two in the morning when Daddy was drunk and fell asleep at the wheel. He hit a side rail, and Mama flew out the windshield, splattering an oak tree at 55 mph. DOA, both of them.

I was sad but not surprised, because Daddy always was a mean, stinky drunk, and Mama was his assistant.

My younger brother Sid was a basket case, and a month later he was married to Penny Gibbs. She sniffed out his insurance money, and exactly one day after the funeral, took him a chess pie, complete with cleavage, and sprayed her scent all over his trail. Sid drooled and fell for it because he was a man.

Penny Gibbs didn't actually murder Sid, but she did set
the stage. Sid died from an overdose of Valium and
whiskey, after a heated argument regarding Penny's whereabouts. Joe Pigg was there in the next room and heard the
whole thing. He found Sid later that night, all curled up
dead on the couch, hugging a bottle of Jack Daniel's. I
know for a fact Penny Gibbs was cheating on Sid, because
I saw her with the mayor out on Paradise Lake Road close
to my lake house. She was all snuggled up next to him like
a teenage girl at a drive-in movie, giggling and kissing his
cheek. Lord knows what her hands were doing.

Penny Gibbs had no conscience and I did admire her
for that. I have always lived on the outskirts of temptation
where it is safe but titillating, always possible to rationalize
my every move.

Take Chester, for instance. Chester is my man, or as
close to a man as I want. He is a Baptist preacher over in
Carter County, and he is married to May, a beautician with
long red fingernails and a two-foot black beehive piled on
top of her head.

Chester comes over every Monday night at nine thirty,
and we sit out in the white wicker swing on my screened-in
back porch, eating lemon icebox pie and listening to "Moon
River," our favorite song. We talk about the Braves, the Bible,
and life. Sometimes Chester takes my chin in his hand, turns
my face toward his, and sings "Moon River" to me.

Chester and I have never even kissed. The closest we
came was two weeks ago when some meringue spilled on
my blouse. He scooped it up with his index finger and
gently touched it to my tongue, holding it there for a
dangerous couple of seconds. We looked at each other
questionably, knowing that a step forward would plunge

us into deep waters. Awkwardly, he removed his finger from my lips, stood up, and said, "I'll see you next week, Darlene." The next week we sat a little farther apart on the swing, and I cleaned up my own spills.

It's best that way.

Here in Mimosa, things never change. Scandals never forgotten, sins never forgiven. What's the payoff? Familiarity, comfort. I've worked at the power company for fifteen years, and will until the day I die. It's enough for me, and I'm proud to know that at the age of thirty-three.

There's no such thing as more.

SHOES GOT UP,
WALKED AWAY ON THEIR OWN
Currie Alexander Powers

The poor old Mississippi is dead today, barely a wave, just one long string of gray muddy water. I know there's life in her somewhere. She's just not showing her face right now.

Johnny Cash wrote one of my favorite songs about her. *And I followed that big river when she called . . .* And that's what I've done, followed the Mississippi all the way down here to New Orleans to find those damn shoes.

I left them here exactly a year ago, tucked under the boardwalk, toes facing the water. A year ago I was sure enough to get rid of things. Now I'm floundering in the kind of emptiness that makes your skin feel like it's hanging on your bones.

I can't throw shoes away when they're done. I retire them. I leave them in a city I like. In the ten years I've been doing this, I've left every pair by a body of water. I guess it's my own desire for freedom that has always seen water as my savior.

Water is always traveling somewhere, moving toward something, the destination, a mystery.

I'm trying to move toward something myself. Damned if I can find it, though.

I'm trying to imagine I can smell the Café Du Monde from where I'm sitting on the lip of the Mississippi at the southern edge of the Quarter. Tourists buzz by in droves like excited insects. Their zeal depresses me.

I've come to the spot. The shoes ain't here. For all I know they got up and walked away on their own.

The women in my family are obsessive about shoes. My father, however, bought the same shoes all his life— Kangaroo-skin ankle boots every two years from a small town hardware store in Northern Ontario.

My mother and my sisters believed variety is the spice of life. We could reminisce for hours about shoes we'd owned: my older sister's haunted green loafers that tapped on the floor at night, my younger sister's beige linen flats with embroidered flowers that once attracted a spider to nest in the toe, my mother's navy and white spectator pumps she said she wanted to be buried in.

A new pair of shoes would be fawned over, everyone doing a Cinderella, taking turns trying them on, envy and admiration weaving us together. Sometimes a pair was given up for adoption when they pinched one's toe and not another's. Shoes were often bought in sets of twins if the style was particularly admired. We could spend hours on the phone with each other describing a pair of shoes we'd seen in a store. Clothes never possessed the personality our shoes did. They were nearly human. We grieved their old age and mourned their passing.

Shoes, to us, were the vestments of our hearts.

In 1963 my mother purchased ten pairs of white

rubber boots in varying sizes for 99¢ a pair, though she only had three children. As I grew, I worked my way up through the sizes, each successively larger number, a graduation from childhood. One pair still exists somewhere, a memento of our pasts.

My mother saved shoes that were decades old. Orange peau de soie pumps from a wedding in 1965, green brocade stilettos with the size written in pencil on the leather sole, the curled toes and worn heels more tangible than any photographic evidence of her life. They had born the weight of her twenties, thirties, forties, the scuffed soles carrying her through time.

Individuality blossomed when my sisters and I started buying our own shoes. Bold choices were a barometer of a new relationship, conservative choices an indication of a new job. Special occasion purchases were like historic markers: the first pair of expensive black pumps, the high-heeled sandals kept in tissue paper in boxes, destined never to suffer the commonness of being everyday shoes, treasured reminders of weddings and parties.

I remember a pair of black needle-nosed shoes I had back in 1985. My sister Joy said they looked "evil." She looked deep in my eyes as if searching for some recent blossoming of blackness in my soul. We went through a period of five years where she seemed to fear my choice in shoes.

The retiring of the shoes is something my older sister, Gail, started. I often think of the green boots she left in a castle in Scotland. I picture their battered soles resting on stone, like fallen soldiers. She lets go of her shoes easier than I do. I take a picture of mine in their final resting place.

My favorite photograph is of the shoes I left in Austin. They were periwinkle blue with four straps across the top with snaps. I loved those shoes. I tried to part with them several times. Five years ago I took them to Austin. I finally found the spot in the park on Town Lake where the statue of Stevie Ray Vaughn stands, looking west. I laid the periwinkle slippers on the bank of the river among some reeds, like Moses in the bulrushes. I liked the idea of Stevie standing guard a few feet away. The picture I took was black and white, the gray tones of the water and the reeds all detail and texture, my shoes, pale appendages, blending into nature as if they grew there. They'd wandered all over North America, walked over pavement and dirt, grass and tile. They finally called it quits in Texas.

I have a ritual I perform at the retirings. I sing some Sam Cooke. *I was born by a river / In a little tent / And like that river / I've been running ever since / It's been a long time coming / But I know / A change is going to come . . .*

It's my theme song. A lot of people think it's a depressing song, but I think it's hopeful. Change will come eventually. It has to.

I've been sitting at the Café Du Monde for an hour. I've had two orders of beignets, and I feel sick. I don't want to go back to my hotel, which is just north of Bourbon Street in the French Quarter. There's an odor that hangs in the air of puke and syrup. It's also noisy. I can't think at night in my hotel room. All I can hear is the bass coming from the club on the corner of Bourbon and Toulouse. Being a musician, I'm obsessed with figuring out what song they're playing just from hearing the bass line. I can't hear much else of the band. They're drowned out by the passing waves of drunk voices. It's truly amazing how excited people can get after seeing a few strippers and drinking a few Hurricanes. It's truly amazing how modesty evaporates in a crowd and women will rip up their T-shirts to expose themselves and grown men throw up on the sidewalk in front of complete strangers.

I need my shoes. I need to see them again. I let go of them too soon. They weren't ready. I wasn't ready. I picture someone walking around with them on, and it makes me anxious.

I need to stay calm. The Café Du Monde is buzzing like a hive. I need indifference. I need to shoe-watch.

I like to see how much I can tell about a person by what they're wearing on their feet. I give scores for taste and originality. I deduct points for wearing sport sandals. I deduct more points if they're wearing them with socks. I admit it, I'm also watching to see if my shoes walk by. I know it's unlikely, but I can't help staring at a bag lady in an orange fright wig as she walks by my table. I see her yellow rubber boots and turn away disappointed.

Maybe later I'll go down to the Central Grocery. All the runaways hang out in front of the fleabag hotel next door. I've seen their tired and hopeless faces. New Orleans is the end of the line for most of them. They've run as far as they can. Maybe one of them wanted to extend the life of my shoes and run a little further.

Shoe details: they were navy blue leather oxfords I bought at the yearly Roots warehouse sale, single eyelet for the laces, leather soles. I dyed them red once, then dyed them black. They were plain shoes, but dependable. The leather soles molded to my feet from years of wearing them. I could slip them on without undoing the laces. I could wear them without socks and they didn't give me blisters. They developed a hole on one side, and I had to put gaffer's tape on the inside so my sock wouldn't stick out. I put one silver stud on either side of the eyelets to dress them up. I had them re-heeled twice. I wore them from Los Angeles to London, from the Yukon to Mexico. They shared eight years of my life. While they were on my feet, I laughed, cried, dreamed, and created. I feel like I've lost a friend.

When I left them on the banks of the Mississippi, I figured I could come back and visit them if I wanted to. And now my life is abridged, lacking in love and inspiration. I picture my shoes under the boardwalk with the brown water flowing past, and I feel vital again. When I went there this morning and they were gone, it felt like a piece of my life had been removed. I'm stalled in one place, but damn it if my shoes aren't traveling without me. I wish they'd taken me with them.

Night falls on the broken sidewalks of Jackson Square. The moon follows me through the streets, a silver ghost, mercury cold. It evaporates into the heat and noise of Bourbon Street as I enter my hotel alone.

It's morning again on the Mississippi. I'm sitting on the bench I left my shoes under. The water shines copper colored, secretive, unwilling to help me. I'm trying to pull something positive out of the situation. I write songs for a living. Here are a few possibilities: "The Ballad Of Louisa's

Lost Shoes," "Lost Soles," "Stepping Out Without My Baby." I'm pathetic. My life has been reduced to looking for shoes that I abandoned a year ago.

I need to see them again, the same way you look at an old photograph and resolve the past.

I can't believe it! I found them. Right there on someone's feet. She's maybe sixteen, very dirty, wearing a Nirvana T-shirt, which is too bizarre in obvious contrast to the life she's currently living. I was standing outside the Central Grocery, eating half a muffeletta, watching the tourists, and there they were, passing right under my nose. I threw the rest of my sandwich away and followed.

I've been following her half the afternoon. She's alone. She talked for a few minutes with some punks outside the hotel. Bummed a smoke and a buck from a tourist couple wearing Hawaiian shirts. It's easy to trail someone in the Quarter. There are crowds on every street. I can keep a discreet distance behind people and still see her feet.

The shoes look awful. The laces are missing and every time the girl takes a step, the tongues flip up like they're gagging from the effort of bending on her feet. She walks east to the edge of the Quarter, down some less busy streets. She walks like she's out on military maneuvers, arms swinging, but her head is down, bouncing on her neck like a rag doll. She has a thick piece of leather tied around one wrist. Her hair is so matted it's converted to dreadlocks. I think I can smell her, like a beagle tracking a fox on the hunt. I feel all jazzed up with adrenaline, secretive, like I'm a spy. She stops to hunt in a garbage can on the corner of Esplanade, and I stop, too, and pretend I'm admiring some flowers inside someone's wrought iron gate. She doesn't find anything and moves on. I follow some more.

I wait outside a bar for nearly an hour when she goes inside. I contemplate going in after her, but I'm afraid to get too close. Maybe she knows I'm following her. I don't want a confrontation yet. The bar is on Decatur, down from the hotel. We've taken a circular route back to where I first saw her. I sit on a bench across the street pretending to read a newspaper. I see her come out of the bar. She heads directly across the street to where I'm sitting. I almost jump up and run, but then I see she's not looking at me. I hide behind the newspaper. Then I feel the bench shift as she sits down.

"You got a dollar for a cup of coffee?"

Her voice cuts right through the mystery of this whole exercise. Suddenly, we're not strangers. I don't look at her while I dig in my pocket. She waits patiently. I stare at the shoes on her feet. Her ankles are creased with dirt. I hand her five dollars 'cause she looks really needy. I swallow a gasp when I see the inside of her arm as she takes the money. Red welts with purple centers, dotted all around the inside of her elbow. A junkie. I close my eyes for a second. I've seen it before. Andy. My favorite guitar player. Rich kid from the suburbs too stretched by his own demons not to try and escape them through the microscopic hole of a needle. He didn't make it out the other side. This girl doesn't look like she will either.

"Thanks," she says in a tired voice.

There's an innocence in the cadence of her words. I want to cry. I see the necklace hanging on the outside of her T-shirt. It has her name spelled out in linked letters of silver. Hope. Then I wonder if it's just her wish, not her name.

She stands up. "Hope?" I say to delay her. "I'm Louisa."

She stares down at me with blank eyes. She smiles, then a look of resignation flattens her face again.

"Thanks," she says and walks off, arms swinging, shoes flapping.

I watch till she's a block away and then I get up and follow. Now that I know her name and she knows mine, I can't let it go. Whatever she is, whoever she is, she has a relationship with my shoes.

I have to keep a bigger distance now. She might recognize me. She hangs around the front of the hotel for most of the night. She goes inside for a couple of hours and then comes back out around ten o'clock. I've been sitting in a café across the street. I have dinner, then dessert, then four cups of coffee. The waiter doesn't seem to mind that I've been there for hours. Hope looks different now. I know she's high. I wonder if my five dollars are in her veins right now. She walks west along Decatur. I pay my bill in a hurry and run after her. She seems to know where she's going, which is more than I can say for myself.

Damn if she doesn't go right down to the river. She walks along the Moon Walk, throwing stones in the water. At one point she even stops right near the spot, and I wonder if she remembers it's the same spot she found the shoes.

She heads off toward the ferry docks after a while, and I move with her. I lose her for a few minutes when the Natchez docks and lets off a stream of tourists. I run around in the crowd, ducking and weaving past people.

Then I see her in the distance, her white T-shirt moving toward the dock where the big ferry takes people to Algiers. I hope she's not going to Algiers. I run past the Natchez toward the dock, and I see her walking down to the water beside the docking slip.

Then I see her starting to climb up the side of the pier, scaling the scaffolding over the water. What the hell is she doing? I stop and watch from a distance. I can just see the swinging dreadlocks and the white T-shirt. The pier is quite high off the ground. The ferry is out at the moment, and the docking slip is a huge, black, empty space. It's quiet except for the sound of water, rolling and sucking, breathing with giant wet lungs. I move closer.

She's made it to the top and is walking along the outside of the structure, hanging onto the wood scaffold. She must not be afraid of heights 'cause she's about two and a half stories up. Now she's out over the water. I get close enough to see the shoreline. It's black and bottomless out there. The waves crash in, then suck the water out again. There's a lot of noise from the water. It's awesome in its power, relentless and hungry.

"Hope!" I yell, but she can't hear me.

She's hanging from the side of the scaffolding by one arm. A wave pulls out and there's a moment of silence as I see her body fall off the side, drifting toward the water, motionless, as if she's already dead. Then I see a small black shape falling beside her body. It's one of my shoes, rocketing down, caught up for a moment when it hits a pole jutting out of the side of the pier. Her body splashes with a surprising lack of eventfulness. Then my shoe splashes in after her. A wave crashes in and then there is nothing.

People come out of nowhere, running, yelling for someone to call the police. Someone from the crowd that just got off the Natchez must have seen her fall. I stand numbly and watch the commotion as people crowd around the edge of the river. A man wades in, but a wave knocks him down and another man has to pull him from the water. I sit down on the pavement. Hope. She didn't have enough.

I wait around till morning. The police come with boats. They drag the harbor when it gets light enough. I leave and come back and they're still dragging the bottom. They don't find her.

I picture her body moving toward somewhere. Just like the river is moving toward somewhere, and I hope she's found peace moving with it. My shoes are going with her, and in that way I feel resolved.

I have dreams, bad dreams for a while after I leave New Orleans. I dream I'm Hope and I'm drowning and the thing that's weighing me down is my shoes, filled with water, leaden, sucking me down to the bottom. Finally I have this dream that my shoes pop loose from my feet and they float to the surface, and then I float to the surface, and as I'm rising in the water, I can see the sun shining up there somewhere and I drift toward it, and I'm anticipating how that first breath of air is going to feel.

PROUST KNEW THE POWER OF AROMA

William W. Fraker

I n early June, the yellow and white petals of honeysuckle
Flower to a chorus of color.
The primrose displays shades of pink.
The pale green cactus on the path to the beach
Arches with ruddy blooms. The verdant Yucca,
With leaves tipped in deep lavender,
Sends an erect stalk straight into the sky,
High off the pavement on the driveway;
A pregnant flag with a pearl colored blossom of promise.
The colors are seen before the overwhelming
Whiff of familiarity consumes the senses.

Proust knew the power of aroma to evoke memory.
The honeysuckle's fragrance triggered a recollection
   of the neighbor
Who introduced me to teasing out the nectar
Of honeysuckle vines while waiting for the school bus
On my way to second grade. This neighbor,
A couple of years older, had just learned to pick
"The Red River Valley" on an acoustic guitar from Sears.

The young singer's mother listened with parental pride
On the porch swing of their Victorian house,

Built a generation before by my grandfather.
This modest white frame house was also the house
My father was born in. My father never really left the place;
He only rented it. It had the nobility of hand built,
Trimmed with a rough carpenter's nod to gingerbread.
A conspicuous bay window on one side of the house
    contained
A sitting place to view the open field in winter.
A round of cement covered the well by the back door.

The frosted glass on the front door bore the image of a stag.
The house sat under a masterful shade oak
    rooted at the end of a sunlit dirt road.
A hedge of crape myrtle in summer turned a brilliant scarlet;
A vigorous greeting to all sweaty visitors.

There is a fading black and white picture in
    the family album
Of my grandmother sitting on the same porch with a banjo
Cradled in her lap. She looks the age of a young bride.
Before the loss of a son to influenza,
    the Depression's stagnation
South of the James, and her painful battle with
    ovarian cancer.
In this photograph, her hair is pulled back tightly,
    her limbs and skirt long,
And her smile reaches into the future. The planking
    and columns of the porch
Must have been her music hall and audience,
    absorbing and echoing
The vibrations of her tunes as meditations of
    celebration and relief;

Pause from a hard life that song provides.
   She probably sang of flowering vines,
Memories of youth, a family's connection to the land,
   and long ago.
Her song can be found in the scent of honeysuckle.

MAMAW AND THE
NIGHT VISITOR
Lonnye Sue Sims Pearson

I t was a typical, sultry Mississippi Delta early summer
night. I had managed to wheedle an invitation to spend
the night with my grandmother. It didn't take much sweet-
talk to get her to tell my parents that I would be staying
over. She just needed a little nudge in the right direction.

Mamaw lived on North Bayou Road directly across
from the Cleveland Country Club in a tiny, nondescript
house that oozed hospitality and love. Surrounded by
roses, honeysuckle, cannas, and nandinas, her house
enticed visits from friends and family alike.

But at night the house was shrouded in darkness. The
back of the property abutted a cotton field, separated by a
flimsy barbed wire fence. Between the fence and the back
door were an orchard and a vegetable garden enclosed in
another barbed wire fence with a lot gate that opened to
the yard. Next to the back door was a rambling rose that
climbed off its lattice frame to clamber over the tiny stoop
and droop thorny tendrils over the steps. If one was tall,
one could get caught in those treacherous thorns. But only
my daddy had to worry about that.

There was a light in the neighboring yard to the south
and a dim streetlight to the north. Neither cast much light
onto Mamaw's little yard, so the back porch was quite dark.

The bedroom that Mamaw and I shared every time I spent the night had a window that overlooked the back steps. Since Mamaw didn't have an air conditioner, we slept in the bed next to the open window. An oscillating fan on the dresser across the room stirred the thick air. The slight Delta breeze carried the sweet smell of roses into the room as Mamaw hummed a hymn to help me go to sleep. Between Mamaw's humming and the warm night air, I almost always fell asleep easily.

One particular night was unusual. The incessant buzzing of the mosquitoes, the heat, and the darkness seemed oppressive. I tossed and turned on the crisp, white sheets that had been dried in the sun that very day. I turned my pillow over several times trying to find a cool spot for my damp neck. Finally I drifted into sleep.

My grandmother was one of a kind. Tall and thin with thick, permed hair that had that hint of blue from beauty parlor bottles, she smelled of lilacs and honeysuckle. She wore stylish shirtwaist dresses that she had made with her own hands and costume jewelry that she had bought wherever she found something she liked. She applied powder and rouge and lipstick carefully every morning whether she was going to work at Kamien's Department Store or not. She always looked the part of the gentle lady that she was. However, underneath all that powder and sweet lilac perfume, there was a tough side to her.

On the aforementioned night, this tough side appeared. At some point in the dead of the night, I awoke to see Mamaw on her knees peering out the window. I sat up, but she waved me down and put a finger to her lips to stop the questions that I wanted to ask. Then I heard it. The sound. At first I couldn't decide if it was an animal or the rustling of the rose canes against the roof. As I strained to hear, the sound moved closer to the house.

Mamaw was crouched low on the bed looking toward the garden. I heard what I thought was the lot gate barely scraping the grass and then stealthy footsteps coming closer in quick bursts. My grandmother's curler-covered head followed the sound straight to the back door.

There was a tentative squeak of the doorknob and then a slight rattle. I held my breath, afraid I would give my grandmother's vantage point away. Then the squeak and rattle became more insistent, and my grandmother slowly raised something up to her shoulder. Quietly, almost in a whisper, she said, "You better go away now. I've got a shotgun pointed at your back, and I'll use it if I have to. Go away now."

She was quite calm and steady. Her voice gave no indication of fear or even anger. But the message was clear.

Immediately, retreating footsteps could be heard returning in the same direction from which they came. Mamaw stared out the window for a few moments, then slowly lowered the gun between the bed and the wall. She turned to me and smiled.

"It's alright now. Go back to sleep."

And believe it or not, I did. After all, Mamaw had everything under control. I doubt if she slept much more that night, but the incident was never discussed in my presence.

The next morning when my grandfather came home from his job as the night watchman at the country club, they whispered to each other for a few minutes in the garden and orchard. Papaw checked the lot gate and walked around to the cotton field.

And that was the end of it.

From that night on, I looked at my grandmother with a new kind of appreciation.

POTTERING AS AN ACT OF GRACE

Ben Norwood

All the tender ministrations given
Annuals whose lives know one season,
All her ordering of tiny objects, valuable
Only to us, perhaps just to her, still
Never left long beyond the loving touch;
The ceaseless cleaning, the rubbings, polish
Applied over and over to furnishings
Old when she was born: her counters
To the ravages of a world in change.
She leaves, against all argument, dead trees
So the woodpecker may have easy pickings.
She saves from the ax every scruffy sapling
Because one day it may amount to shade
Or give cover to migrating birds.
She plants too many tulips, dresses fur bearing
Animals against winter, and feeds all the strays.

She gives rearrangement without number
To furnishings satisfactory where they are
In pursuit of a perfect place, harmony
Of objects and inhabitants, a respite
From welter, from the hurry of getting.

She's unwilling to turn loose of the worn,
The scrap of fabric kept too long, a car
Driven beyond any engineer's expectation.

Her life's an investment of love
In the passing, in all the world's flotsam
And jetsam that come her way, sidle up
To her touch, rest under her eye, secured
For an instant, saved for a second
From randomness, and endowed with value.

Each meager object or creature shares a love
Unbidden, perhaps undeserved, that imbues
Them with a glow deeper than her polish,
Whose origin they can't find in themselves,
But whose effects are undeniable, myself
Chief among those plucked from the random.

COLORING OUTSIDE THE LINES
Linda Therber

The small patterns are sorted, stacked, and stored in the sewing basket she no longer uses, little squares, triangles, circles cut from brown paper grocery sacks so many years ago. Once pinned to scraps of everyday clothes, worn-out shirts, to flour sacks stamped with sailboats or nosegay bouquets, waiting to take shape on her bed's chenille spread, they are now put away.

Sometimes I pinned the patterns, following admonitions to "put them close together," and "turn the triangles this way and that way to make the most of what you have." When I was old enough, I graduated to cutting. "Mind your edges and borders," she'd say. "Stay on the line. Don't cut into the pattern."

The brown paper shapes were pocked with pinholes punched again and again in the same direction until each piece assumed a front and a back and transcended itself. The front side, pocked with dot-to-dot pictures or points on an unlined roadmap. The back, bumpy with rimmed pinpricks, Braille text of unwritten stories, testimony to hours and hours of a woman's toil.

When I held a pattern toward window light, pinholes twinkled like star chart dots in a third grade science book. The Big Dipper on this one. Orion's Belt on that one. On others, unnamed, earthbound constellations of womenfolk and their work.

The paper patterns grew soft and worn as bits and pieces of who we were, of what we'd been, were scrapped together, and the remnants of our lives were whole, unfolding to warm us, spread summer picnics, pad straw for autumn hayrides, hide worn seats of a '51 Ford Victoria.

I'd sit on the couch beside her as she sewed, an emerging quilt puddled in her lap, a coloring book resting in mine.

"Let me see what you've done," I'd say, my way of securing a chance to show what I'd done, to fish for compliments.

I offered no praise for the handiwork she showed me. She was the adult, the parent, the nurturer. I was the child, self-centered, wanting attention, holding up a coloring book picture for the approval she always gave.

"Very nice," she'd say, not mentioning the wayward paths my crayons took, not pointing out mistakes, not declaring, "You colored outside the lines," but instead offering direction and encouragement. "Very nice. Be sure to mind your lines and edges and color me another pretty picture."

I was a good student. I learned to mind my edges and improved until I could outline a picture in black or a contrasting color, solid proof that I understood boundaries and colored inside the lines.

Then a spring came when, with fingertips needled by a winter's quilting, she put away the scissors, the patterns and pins, her skin too thin to work a needle against it, her hands too tired to guide the thread.

"My hands need a rest from sewing," she said, "but I want to keep them busy. I've thought about it. I want a coloring book. Do they make them with pictures of flowers or birds?"

"I'll find one," I say.

"I need crayons, too."

"I'll get them."

We sit side-by-side on her couch, coloring books in our laps. The monarch butterfly I've colored is outlined in black.

She holds up her page, shows it to me. "What do you think?"

"Very nice," I say, looking at the rose she colored, the red of its petals feathered beyond their outline. "Very nice. Let's color another pretty picture."

She smiles and returns to her work.

Boundaries have shifted. Borders are changed. Like the brown paper shapes stored away, she and I are wrinkled and worn, trying to find the lines, mind our edges, make the most of what we have—coloring outside the lines.

MOTHER'S HANDS IN CHURCH
Nelda Rachels

Calloused from milking the cow,
Mother's hands played the notes
her ears, tone deaf, could not follow.
The hymnal, light as churned butter,
lay in her lap, while "Just As I Am"
bawled against stained glass.

While the preacher's words stroked
the pews ahead, my mother's hands
embraced like timid lovers in a quiet room.
Sometimes, I'd lean into my mother's
side and pull on fingers that knew
the quilter's needle or crochet hook:
"Flower Garden" warmed my parents' bed
and DaVinci's "The Lord's Supper," in cream
crochet the size of feed-sack twine,
filled a six by four foot frame above our couch.

The lowing of prayer was my call
to dreams and the slow release of Mama's
hands on mine. Her hands slipped to a sweaty
grip on hoe and the tired chop-chop
of weeds that have echoed from Garden

to garden, from green bean row to green
bean row since Eve forced the curse.
The curse passed to me as well, dirt under
my fingernails and hands jarring as hoe
hit hard ground and nicked
tomato plant instead of weed.

Mama sent me to the kitchen sink,
a safer place, she hoped, till a glass shattered
against the tap and cut my tense hands.
"There's power in the blood, the wonder
working blood" stirs me and sends
my mother's thumbs in dance, circular
do-si-dos on top of her closed hymnal.
While her hands play, my own grip
the pew, then search her warmth again.

THE SWEETEST WORD
Connie Foster

I was fifty-one years old when the cattle truck rolled on top of my brand new VW Beetle. Squashed it like a bug. It was an impulsive gift to myself. At the time I suffered from a bad case of empty nest syndrome, and my sunny yellow convertible was meant to replace something irreplaceable— the day-to-day routine of mothering.

What started with the smell of freshly mown onions on a cloudless eighty-degree day ended with traumatic brain injury, a crushed pelvis, and a severed spine. The twisted, torn bodies of cattle strewn across the highway seemed surreal. Even now, the sound of their bawling serves as the background music of my nightmares.

As I lay on the operating table in an anesthetic blur, I remember hearing someone say, "We nearly lost her." My rebellious nature kicked in, and I wanted to slap someone. My brain screamed, "Are you crazy? I'm too young to die." When I became fully aware of my condition, I discovered the doctors had brought me back but left my body behind.

My face is now a puzzle of missing pieces, my body a rag doll of inanimate parts. Communication works one way. I can receive input, but I can't bitch back. In the moment it took a small herd of cattle to teeter their load, my fit, well-maintained body became this unrecognizable creature with little left, save one good arm. Thanks for nothing, Doc.

I spent three and a half weeks in a hospital, followed by three months in rehab before they sent me back to my house. Every day my eyes pleaded to go home, but I discovered it was way too soon. My husband was terrified. Still is.

This place isn't really home anymore. It looks like home, minus some rugs and furniture, plus a couple of ramps and a remodeled bathroom. It looks like home, but it doesn't feel like home. I can't do what I used to do. I can't feel the warmth of freshly laundered towels. I can't feel the soapy suds of warm dishwater. I can't feel buttermilk biscuit dough squishing between my fingers. I can't feel my rear on the cold toilet seat. This place isn't home. It's a burning torment. My real home is this effing wheel chair, where time is measured by diaper changes.

I miss so many little things from my former life, like the sound of my own voice, late morning sex on Saturdays, the tirades of my Oprah-loving book club, gift wrapping in the middle of the living room floor, and calling friends and talking about nothing, talking about everybody. I miss that husband who never had to fake his contentment. I miss my daughter who slips further away each day.

My husband and I live in a gunless house, where knives and medications are stored on the top shelf. He sold the guns, and the other accomplices to my futile attempts at suicide are now out of reach.

Before my accident, the man couldn't keep his hands off me, had to have it at least twice a week or he claimed to get "the jitters." He wasn't joking. I look at him now, and I see muscles twitching and the nervous dance of his left eye. He puts a finger on the Parkinsoned lid, but it's no use.

He lets go and it continues its dance. Please God, give me my voice back for five seconds so I can tell him to go out and get a little.

He's a good man, but he was much better at being cared for than care giving. Maybe I'm not the only reason he got rid of the guns. I fear for him as I watch time distort his features, with each day tally marked down the side of his face. I fear for me as every day brings the worry that he might leave me for another woman or another world.

Eight months after the crash, my daughter married a young man she had been engaged to for twenty-one months. I hadn't liked him very much until my accident. He came to the hospital every day, not only for my daughter, but also for me. He read to me, fed me, talked about someday becoming a daddy. It broke what little was left of my heart when he died. They had just celebrated their first anniversary when his truck got in the way of someone else's accident. For my family, seems getting behind the wheel is as deadly as Russian roulette.

"Dead on impact," the police had said.

Lucky bastard, I thought.

Watching my daughter plan and carry out her wedding without my help was tough, but watching her suffer such a loss without my comfort was unnatural. I wanted to die all over again. We all did. But one thing got us through. She was five months pregnant.

I'll never forget the day of the birth. My daughter had insisted I be there during the delivery. Besides the doctor, I was the first one to see my new grandbaby, to count her tiny toes and fingers, to reach out with my good arm and rub her naked, slimy tummy. What a thrill to see the birth of that precious life that had given us all a reason to live!

During what I thought would be a time of great joy, my daughter's spirit evaporated, sucked dry by postpartum depression. All I could do was watch her slide, like a load of cattle crashing toward me in slow motion.

Lately, every time I see my beautiful grandbaby, she's dressed in a dingy, frayed sweater. Somebody needs to tell my daughter that she's roasting that baby. Doesn't she realize it's the middle of summer? Her visits to my house are down to once a week on Saturdays. However, by my calculations from overheard conversations here and there, she sees her in-laws about three times a week. At times I've hated them for it, my daughter included. Even now, my jealousy and insecurity can destroy my good sense, like a young girl scratching and pulling the hair of her best friend over some silly boy. Such raw emotions are hard to control, but I'm trying. They say the first step to recovery is admitting the truth, so here it goes. I've been replaced by the mother-in-law.

I've seen my granddaughter with this woman three times. During the first visit, their game of teddy bear peek-a-boo made me think the unthinkable—*I'd like to shove that teddy bear up Grandma's ass.* After the second visit, I thought, *Fool, can't you see that hole in her sweater? Get off your fat rump and buy that baby some new clothes.* But on the third visit, I was finally able to see through the fog of my jealousy and realize that my precious granddaughter needed this woman in her life. If only God would give me my voice and two good arms for just one minute, I'd shake some sense into my daughter and tell her this child can't afford to lose another parent.

My grandbaby is now eleven months old, and she hates me. Or maybe she's afraid of me. No wonder. What child wouldn't be frightened of a pathetic, crippled woman who can't talk, who has a nasty bag of disgusting stuff hanging off the side of her wheelchair and no toy in sight. This isn't a grandma's house. Grandma's houses have stuffed animals, games, books, and snacks in the shape of Sponge Bob Square Pants. I was a primary school teacher for twenty-three years before my accident, but there isn't a children's book in my house. I've bought hundreds over the years, all left in my classroom, or what used to be my classroom, awaiting my return.

Today, I made up my mind to do something about it. I wanted to be prepared for their weekly visit, because I couldn't get my mind off those loose threads eating across the cable knit weave of my granddaughter's sweater. For weeks I've watched that hole grow bigger and bigger, like the hole that separates me from her. If I let the raveling continue, I'm afraid I'll lose her forever.

Opening the door, I rolled my motorized chair down the ramp. The warmth of the sun made me even more determined. My husband followed with a frantic look on his face.

"Where are you going?" he asked.

When I continued to roll down the driveway and onto the sidewalk, he yelled again, "Where are you going?"

Stupid questions really piss me off. He knows I can't answer, so why ask?

I stopped the chair and motioned with my good arm for him to follow. When I got to the end of the block, he pleaded for me to turn around.

"Let's go back, and I'll get the van. We can go wherever you like."

I kept going. I knew he would not take me wherever I

liked, and I could never get him to understand where I needed to go. He began to panic, and I must admit, I found it amusing. This will teach him, teach him to get me out every now and then, and I don't mean hidden away inside the van. Maybe now he'll stop treating me like my mind is as crippled as my body.

I continued on and he followed, past Madge Underhill's lily garden, past Ruth Wilson's yard with the tacky lawn ornaments peeing on her marigolds, past Speedy's Auto Parts painted in black-and-white blocks like the checkered flag you hope to see at the finish line. We traveled over a mile to get to The Bookmark Book Store.

I pulled on the door, and my husband opened it for me. I rolled forward just inside the entrance and breathed in the smell of print. It felt like coming home. When I found the children's section, the first book I picked up was *Brown Bear, Brown Bear, What Do You See?* by Eric Carle— a keeper. I handed it to my husband and reached for another. I flipped through a few Clifford books but decided against them. Never did like that dog. But I had to have *Where Is Baby's Belly Button?* and *Grandma and Me*, both by Karen Katz.

I motioned my husband to the checkout counter. He paid, and we exited the building. He didn't say a word as we made our way back home. No more stupid questions. A light breeze tickled the hair that grazed my neck, and a smile curled my lips.

When we returned home, my husband changed my colostomy bag, fed me a handful of pills, and lifted me out of my wheelchair and into his leather recliner, normally considered sacred territory. He placed the bag of books on my left side, and we waited.

They arrived. My grandbaby was wrapped around her mother's legs. Her grandpa unlocked her little hands, pulled her off my daughter, and placed her in my lap.

"What are you doing?" my daughter asked. "And why is Mom in your chair?"

He didn't say a word.

I expected my grandbaby to cry, but she didn't. She sat on my dead legs, frozen in terror. I reached down and lifted a book out of the bag and placed it in front of her where she could easily see the bear on the front cover. She picked up the book, and her body seemed to soften.

"Read to Grandma," my husband said.

She turned each page, one at a time, and named every animal. What a smart girl to be talking at such a young age! When she finished, I reached over and picked up another. She turned through a few pages, then lifted her shirt, playing with her belly button. I looked up at my husband and daughter, both smiling. She put that book to the side and hopped off my lap to empty the shopping bag. Hugging the last book to her little chest, she tried to climb back onto my lap.

My daughter walked over, boosted her up, and read the title of the last book. "Grandma and Me."

The precious baby in my lap carefully examined each page, unaware of the emotional chaos she wheeled between the adults in the room. There was no screaming, no reaching for the door, no hiding behind Mama's legs. Just my grandbaby and me.

After running her tiny hand across the last page, she closed the book and turned her face to mine. Her ruby lips puckered, and she called me something I had never been called before.

"Grandma," she said.

It was the sweetest word.

PLAY IT AS IT LAYS
Ben Norwood

I t's a dictum from golf.
The guys in bright outfits
Got it right, at least once.
Though they missed the grammar.

Play it where it landed.
Do whatever you must:
Knock it out of the knot hole,
Wade into the water,
Choke up down to the steel shaft.

Just take it as it comes,
And ask no mercy,
Mercy not always forthcoming.
Play it as it lies. Face

The phenomena, beat 'em back.
It's you versus randomness,
You versus human intent,
You versus your worst enemy,
Your own mistakes.

The whole cause and effect
Universe has unraveled for all
History just to land you here.
And now, you, my boy,
Must play your way out.

For Zachery Douglas Norwood

TRADE DAY
Kory Wells

S herrie had been in bed for the better part of a week. She knew she wasn't as bad off as some of those people on Montel and Dr. Phil, but still. She was in a funk and she couldn't seem to pull out of it. She hadn't been sleeping much at all. She'd been lying there making these lists in her head. Lists of all the things that had gone wrong in her life.

At the top was the fact that she'd lost her job, her good job, at Odom's Food Town two weeks ago. Paulette Jefferson had tried to return a half-eaten package of double-stuffed Oreos, saying she had bought them the week before and they were already stale. Sherrie knew this was Paulette's latest method of stretching her food budget. It wasn't much better than out-and-out shoplifting, which Sherrie had suspected Paulette of a time or two. In the past few weeks, she'd exchanged Paulette's half-empty packages of oyster crackers, potato chips, and Cheerios for brand new ones. Sherrie had rolled her eyes at all of those things, but double-stuffed Oreos was going too far. She didn't know what took hold of her, but she let loose on Paulette.

The only thing she remembered saying for certain was "To hell with this customer's-always-right shit." She never had liked Paulette anyway. Or Paulette's no-count, snotty-nosed kids who came in the store barefoot and drank out of the co-cola bottles before they paid. Sherrie told her that, too. Randall Odom came in on the tail end of the conversation and fired Sherrie on the spot. Mrs. Miles, the other cashier, reported that Paulette went home with a new package of double-stuffed Oreos plus a gallon of milk on account of her trouble. Sherrie went home with half a paycheck and a headache.

The next thing on Sherrie's list went way back, to that mess with her PE teacher, Mr. Blanton, when she was eight. And nine and ten. Of course she didn't know it was a mess then. She only knew it didn't feel right to touch him when they were alone in the old locker room of her elementary school. But he offered her candy and little girl gifts like lip gloss and stickers, and so she petted it like he asked her. She tried not to look at it. One time she watched his face, and it flinched around like the rest of him. Like he was working up to a big sneeze. But instead of sneezing, he closed his eyes and grunted like he had stubbed his toe. After that Sherrie kept her eyes off Mr. Blanton altogether. Instead she studied the towers of cardboard boxes and junk that surrounded them like strange ancient ruins she had seen in her classroom encyclopedias.

The locker room had served as a storage room and dump for years. It smelled like musty cardboard and moldy sneakers. When Mr. Blanton finished jerking, he would tuck it in, zip up, and give Sherrie an old rag to wipe her hands on. The rag was a stiff pile of wrinkles, like it had been starched in a heap. Sherrie rubbed her hands on the rough edge, then handed the rag back. After that pathetic attempt at hygiene, Mr. Blanton always asked, "You want to look in a box?"

She would pick one to open, sometimes one up high

that he would lift down for her. When she pulled back the flaps, a visible puff of particles rose up and made her cough. Sometimes the box would have old textbooks or a scrap heap of supplies, but at other times she found costumes, instruments, play dishes, and crayons that were hardly used at all. At Mr. Blanton's urging, she took home her favorite finds.

That went on until fifth grade, right before Sherrie's eleventh birthday. Mrs. Carlisle, the first grade teacher, walked into the locker room looking for a butterfly costume for a play. Sherrie was digging through a box of old board games and puzzles. She didn't notice Mr. Blanton move to an innocent-looking distance away.

"I've been watching her for some time now," she heard him say. "I suspect she's been stealing." Sherrie's eyes and mouth both rounded into "ohs." Now, years later, her eyes narrow but her nostrils still round out in those same "ohs" when she thinks about him.

Her daddy whipped her for bringing all that stuff home, after which her mama said, "Don't come running to me." They never asked how she came to be in that old locker room in the first place. After that she went from one mess to the next. Smoking. Drinking. Getting detention. Getting expelled. Getting laid. Getting pregnant. Her marriage to Bobby Little didn't last. He stayed around long enough to knock her up one more time. Left her with two babies, no car, the rent due, and no milk in the fridge. She took the few belongings she could afford to part with—a black-and-white TV, a chenille bedspread, a shaggy orange bath mat, and an anniversary candle that Bobby's grandmother had given them—and went to Trade Day. She came home with milk money and Hugh.

Hugh was a flea market dealer. He worked all the shows and trade days in the tri-state area. Scottsboro, Acworth, and more little towns than Sherrie could keep straight, plus the big-city shows in Nashville, Atlanta, and Birmingham. He made a decent living for them, but he was gone all the time. So it was up to her alone to make a mess of her kids, raising them in Hugh's overflowing duplex.

All of Hugh's junk was on another of Sherrie's lists, the list of everything she'd like to throw out. Hammers, ratchet sets, drill bits. Broken down washing machines and dryers. The single car garage and the spare bedroom were full of junk when she moved in. Vacuums, sewing machines, ropes, and God knew what else. She had to move some of it into the dining room to make room for the kids' beds. Hugh bitched at her for weeks about moving his stuff, so she never touched it again. Now every room was filled. In twenty years, he hadn't hauled the first thing away. If it didn't sell after a few weeks, he brought it home and piled it up. You couldn't open the front door for boxes of imported plastic clothespins, bouncy balls, and multi-colored umbrella hats from China. Those imports from China were Hugh's latest craze. Buy in quantity, sell in quantity. It was the future, he said.

Now here she was with no job and nothing to do but look at all his junk. A couple of days was all it took before she had to go to bed.

When Hugh came home a few days after that, she got up and stood in front of the TV while the announcer was talking about NASCAR. That got Hugh's attention, but she didn't get the answer she was hoping for.

"When I'm home, I don't want to be cleaning. I want to be spending time with you, babe," he said.

"You spend more time with that TV than with me," she said, and went back to bed.

She was done spending time with him. She was done spending time here on earth, period.

So for the last few days she'd been making a new list. A list of ways to kill herself. Her first idea was to blow her brains out, but the messy part stopped her. She could imagine putting a gun to her head and pulling the trigger, but she couldn't leave the aftermath for Hugh. Or the kids, if by some next to impossible chance they happened to come visit before Hugh discovered her body. There was also the problem that she didn't own a gun and didn't know a thing about them. What was she going to do, walk into a pawn shop and say, "What kind of gun do you have that would be good for killing a person at close range?" She didn't think so. No gun, no blast of relief.

Next she considered an overdose. That was nice and neat, but she was scared she wouldn't get the job done, and then where would she be. She was too chicken to hang herself. Didn't want to do anything painful. Didn't have a gas oven. Gas. She recalled stories of people putting themselves to sleep in a car left running in a closed garage. It sounded painless. Neat and clean.

The only problem was the stuff in the garage. But she wouldn't have to clean it all out. Just enough to pull in the car.

Sherrie got out of bed and went into the kitchen to splash water on her face. She didn't want to risk seeing herself in the bathroom mirror. Out the kitchen window she saw that the sky was a deep, heavenly blue. Fourth Saturday in October. Hugh was gone to Nashville for the weekend. She had plenty of time.

Although the day was cool, she worked up a sweat hauling all the junk out into the yard. Picture frames, bottomless chairs, old motors, and parts, parts, parts. Pots and pans. Used steel-toed work boots. Shoeboxes of marbles and yo-yos and punch-out paper gliders. Before long she had an area big enough for the car cleared out. Except for the heavy stuff.

Two Kenmore washing machines and an avocado Westinghouse upright freezer stood between Sherrie and eternity. She pushed and pulled and grunted and nearly peed in her pants from the strain. She could rock them a little, but that was it. She leaned over one of the Kenmores and admired the empty concrete in front of her. She hadn't seen such an expanse of empty floor in years. It made her giddy. She wondered if she drove the car into the garage at a high speed whether she could push the machines out of the way. But no, that would probably attract the neighbors' attention and then her plan wouldn't work.

A faded blue Ford F150 pulled into her driveway and two women got out and walked up in matching Goodwill tennis shoes. Both of them had dark greasy hair strung flat across their heads so their scalps peeked through. They were obviously sisters, maybe twins. Their dresses flared and swayed like bells from their substantial hips.

"We's just driving by and saw your sale," the heavier one said to Sherrie. "Looks like you've got a lot of good stuff."

Sherrie started to say, "This ain't no sale," but she looked at the mess in the yard and stopped herself.

"Make me an offer," she said. "It all needs to go."

These are hefty women, she thought, as they browsed through the junk. The three of them together could push those machines out of the way. The three of them together could move a bunch of this stuff. These women didn't look hungry, but they looked like they could use a little extra pay. Payment in goods, maybe, but Sherrie had some cash, too. Hugh always left her with plenty of cash. Or these women might be dealers. They had a truck. They could haul this stuff off. To Trade Day, to their own house, to the dump. It didn't matter as long as it was out of her way.

Sherrie walked toward the women as they inspected a box of old jars and bottles. In dingy white fake Nikes with a not-quite-right blue swish, her feet seemed to glide across the gravel drive. This was the most purpose she had felt in days. Weeks. Maybe years. Her feet were so light, she felt like running. Or skipping. Or turning a cartwheel, God forbid. She still had enough sense to know she'd hurt something if she tried that. As she reached the women, two more cars pulled up at the curb. A skinny man in a plaid Western dress shirt and a Mexican couple with two young children walked up.

"If you like this junk, this is just the tip of the iceberg," Sherrie announced to them all. "And this is your lucky day. I want to make you a deal." She felt a smile rise up from her gut. Hugh was going to be so mad. But he wasn't going to have to clean up the mess.

WANDA'S FRIED CHICKEN
Thomas D. Reynolds

The song ends, but Joe doesn't know it,
frail arms and legs still pecking away
putting a new spin on the "Funky Chicken"
as danced to forties big band standards.
DANCE NIGHT AT THE FONTANA CIVIC CENTER.

Joe may not know when the ax falls,
at least if Death taps his bony shoulder.
May think he's trying to muscle in on his woman,
her with the mustache and support hose,
arthritic hands, and labored breath.
"If that's Death, let him get his own chick,"
Joe might say. "Take old Wanda Davis,
starved like a pullet for fifteen years.
Grab a wrinkled spur or bald wing
and dance a quick rumba to the bone yard,"
he tells Death, catching Wanda's gaze
as she considers throwing him a bone,
imagining what he would look like naked,
picturing an old plucked rooster
with sagging comb and barely able to cluck,
let alone crow, and tough to boot.

"Dinnertime!" she yells, and the floor clears,
a skyful of hawks swoops in for the plates.
Golden perfection: legs, thighs, and breasts.
Joe eats with almost cannibalistic glee,
Wanda believes, the ancient cock of the walk,
walking bandy-legged back to his bloated pullet,
Rhode Island Red with high-pitched cluck.
How many eggs can she lay in one sitting?
Wanda imagines Joe as one of the yardbirds
squawking and scrambling in her coop,
flapping his dumb wings to save his life.
Then quickly, to benefit all womankind,
he's undone at the neck, left to flop,
drained, singed, dressed, soaked, and fried.

But at least he's a rooster, she considers,
and not Jack Spoon, the Great Horned Owl,
hooting an old jibe to get her attention,
with his cowlick and big round spectacles.
At least Joe could stir up a little dust
in the henhouse, and crow in the new day.
Let them fight it out behind the elevator,
with hay bales for stands and pits of straw.
Joe could be the fat end of my wishbone,
Wanda thinks, suddenly catching Joe's gaze
as he admires her delicate shank and wattle,
the way she roosts without a single cackle,
her eyes like two gravel bits burning
a fiery path to his gizzard and craw.

KNOCKS OF THE OPPORTUNISTIC
AND HARD KINDS
Kristin O'Donnell Tubb

You know those cords they lay across a highway to see if there's enough traffic there to expand the road, or to at least add a turn lane? Well, my momma to this day will tell you those aren't counters, those are speed traps that somehow trigger as you run over them, and so every time she runs over one, she slams on the brakes so hard the anti-lock system kicks in. As if braking *after* running over them if they *were* speed traps would do you any good, anyhow.

But that's not the point. Point is, Big Jim Gilliam (no relation to Julie, she says, but talk around town puts them at second cousins) owned a two-bit used car lot— eloquently named Big Jim's Used Car Lot—on County Road 68 just past the Ripe-n-Ready and the Beauty School. Since business was booming around that area, the Mayor (whose brother ran the largest bootlegging ring in the state, or at least in East Tennessee, down that very same stretch of road) decided to put "wonna them counters" down across 68.

Big Jim, hearing opportunity knock, filled up his blue Nissan truck with gas, chocolate covered donuts, and a gallon of chocolate milk. For five straight hours every night, Big Jim would cruise south down 68 to the Sweet

Love Southern Baptist Church, turn around in the parking lot, head back up 68, then swing through Bill Cartwright's circular drive to complete the loop.

See, Big Jim just knew if 68 got expanded to a four-laner, he'd pull in money from as far away as Polk County. So he'd pop Patsy Cline or Willie Nelson or Hank Williams (Senior—always Senior) in the tape player and cruise. On Fridays and Saturdays, he'd replace that chocolate milk with a little Jim Beam and bellow, "He's a Bigger Jim than me, alright!" He'da gotten away with everything, too, if it hadn't been for Bill Cartwright getting fed up to here with Big Jim's headlights shining through his bedroom window every four minutes.

So Cartwright took that shotgun off the wall which is really supposed to be just for show and shot out Big Jim's back left tire. Big Jim was so cheap that he drove on the rim for another half-mile just to make it over that counter one more time.

Sheriff Tuggle was none too happy to find out about Big Jim's scheme and threatened to throw him in jail for tampering with a crime scene. Sheriff Tuggle knew that the "tampering" part was right but wasn't too positive what else to call a cord that lays across the road, and since "tampering with the crime scene" was the first thing that popped into his mind 'cause of that Matlock episode last night, he decided to call Big Jim's bluff.

Big Jim bought it and whimpered like a baby until it occurred to him to bribe Sheriff Tuggle, since that's what that guy did on Matlock last night. Big Jim laid it out for Sheriff Tuggle like this: since no one knew how many times *he* had run over that cord and how many times *real* passers-by had, if Sheriff Tuggle would just forget about this little incident, Big Jim'd be sure and cut the boys down at the station a deal on a new-used Chevy with one hell of a V-8, wink-wink.

Sheriff Tuggle was a man used to being offered gifts, and probably would've considered the offer further had his own momma not lived on 68. But he couldn't stand the thought of widening this road and allowing all them Polk County hoodlums to travel right by her house—not that she wasn't a good shot. So, putting on his best state of appall, he scoffed at Big Jim's offer, cuffed him, and threw him in jail until the next morning.

Now, had Sheriff Tuggle arrested Big Jim for DUI (which he could've) or bribery (which he should've), the next chain of events would've never happened. But no, Sheriff Tuggle had his mind set on that tampering charge and booked him. The next day, Big Jim sobered up, was released, and went to Riddle & Wallace drugstore for a lemonade—he was a little dehydrated, after all. Eddie McMillan, the town's poorest lawyer, just so happened to be there and overheard Big Jim relaying the previous night's events to Tammi, the store clerk/beauty consultant. Well, *he* heard opportunity knocking and set to convincing Big Jim to sue the polyester pants off that no-good Sheriff of ours. Can't charge that, you see. You'll be rich, you see. Big Jim bought it and a lemonade for Eddie to boot.

A few days after Eddie filed suit, the county attorney called Sheriff Tuggle with strict instructions to settle, settle, settle. Eddie McMillan drives one of those Buick Celebrities these days (compliments of Big Jim's Used Car Lot), and wears the fanciest ties you ever did see, with little bottles of Tabasco on them, or little Santa Clauses at Christmastime, or little UT's on game days.

Big Jim invested his winnings in enough concrete to make a 100-yard turn lane right in front of Big Jim's Used Car Lot. Business picked up that first day, but only because everyone wanted to write their names in the cement. What is it about being immortalized in mortar?

But that's not the point. Point is, I suppose, you can't count on progress. Nothing's set in concrete. Least that's what my momma would say.

BIRDCAGE KINCAID
Neil O. Jones

I t was late August when T-Bone and I saw him coming
to football practice that day on his bicycle. I was the
first to notice there was something different about him.
"Well, I'll be durn, T-Bone," I said as I pointed down
Denley Drive. "Looka there at your boy."

Tommy Kincaid's upper body was going up and down
and side-to-side as he pumped his bike. The change stood
right out. He had a face guard on his helmet. HE HAD A FACE
GUARD! Nobody—man or boy—had a face guard playing
football in the late 1950's in Dallas. This was sacrosanct
Texas football where every boy learned to get his face
plowed in the ground and like it, or at least act like it didn't
hurt that much even when it did. And here was this guy
with vertical and horizontal bars to protect his hawk face.

T-Bone stood still and squinted and held a hand over
his eyes to shade the blazing sun. Kincaid made his way
closer. Then as T-Bone saw what he couldn't believe he was
seeing, his jaw dropped. "Say it ain't so," T-Bone told me.
"Looks like a beady-eyed bird staring out a cage." At that
moment, the nickname "Birdcage" took flight and clasped
on to Kincaid forevermore.

At twelve years old, weighing a mere 125 pounds, but
towering at 6 feet 3 $\frac{1}{2}$, Tommy Kincaid stood a head or two

above the rest of us. He was in junior football, the Oak Cliff Jets, with T-Bone, me, and others. It was the combination of his hawk nose and beady eyes behind that football face mask that emphasized his avian-like markings. But his most noticeable feature was his ears that stuck out half-round and large like grapefruit halves stuck on the sides of his head. And we knew he could out hear a dog with them, as he caught us a few times talking about him from thirty yards away. He was gangly and awkward on the field and off.

Thinking back on it, we all stood out in our own way on the football field. On our backs we had our large red playing number on our white jerseys. On the front we had our number smaller at the left shoulder with most of the front reserved for our sponsors. Several companies kicked in for our equipment, and I guess it worked out with one sponsor per man. T-Bone displayed "Mullins Service Station, We Aim to Please," but the lettering was too much, and it hung too low, and the last part was tucked in his pants. It came out "Mullins Service Station, We Aim." I sported "Chief's Radiator Service" above a drawing of an attacking Indian, mouth open wide in a war whoop and tomahawk raised high above his head. My ad also was too long, with just the top of the tomahawk poking out from the top of my pants. Birdcage had "Dudley M. Hughes Funeral Home" on the front of his shirt. And every bit of it showed. Coach Wilkins couldn't remember the names of so many players, so he called us by a shortened version of our sponsor. T-Bone was Mull, I was Chief, and Birdcage was Dud.

At practice that day on the Lisbon School ball field, when Birdcage wasn't playing, he was watching the scrimmage, standing on the sideline with his arms crossed and his hands cupped over his elbows. He was always standing on one leg or the other. The resting leg was crossed at his ankle like a pink yard flamingo. That day he started the habit of always having his helmet on, and it was so hot that the Vitalis hair oil on his red hair melted and was greasing down and glistening on his forehead and the back of his neck. Pride in that fence-faced helmet must have let him clean forget it was August and he was in Texas. I watched in fascination as he stuck his fingers through the side holes of his helmet so he could pull it apart wide enough to get it off and swab his greasy brow with his sleeve.

"You reckon he is right proud of them face bars?" I asked T-Bone. "Watch him squeeze that helmet right back on again."

And he did.

"Hey! Birdcage!" I yelled at him. He owled his head around a quarter-turn without moving his body.

"What do you want, man?" he said in that tinny, nasal voice.

"Aw, nothing," I told him. Then in a lower tone I said to T-Bone. "See there, he's cross-eyed as he can be, a looking around each side of that middle up-and-down bar."

"I heard that!" Birdcage said.

T-Bone had been quiet, studying Birdcage. After a little bit, he leaned over and said low to me, "Walk over behind him with me and watch this. I'm gonna pop the top off that bottle."

Kincaid had just watched the punter on the field kick a high one. He had his head laid back with his face almost horizontal to the sky. Perfect, it turned out, for T-Bone's move. With one quick, fluid motion from behind, T-Bone jerked the snap open on Kincaid's helmet and with his other hand reached over the head to get a handful grip on the face mask. Just as quickly, he ripped the helmet off and tossed it to me. Instinctively, I caught it.

I wondered what that first sensation was like for Kincaid. He would have felt his helmet jerk left at the pop of the right snap. Then the four snaky fingers, or eight if he really was cross-eyed, appearing from the sky and closing off his vision as they curled through the bars and rubbed his face before they locked on. Then the violent rip and his head snapping back, trying to ease the pressure as the helmet raked over the Dumbo ears.

He bent over and bobbed up and down, holding his ears with his hands while making a strange, high-pitched kind of screeching sound. As Birdcage wheeled around and straightened up, still holding both ears, the first person he saw was T-Bone, grinning and pointing at me. I stood there holding the helmet out in front of me like a scalp.

"You . . . you . . . that hurt, man," he blurted out at me and yanked his helmet back. "You do that again and I'm telling Coach." That statement, I thought to myself, proved he should have his ears boxed regularly. Justifiable ear ripping, if ever such a thing existed.

I started to explain—then I stopped. There was no use telling him I didn't do it. I was, first of all, just dang sorry enough to have done it if I had thought of it, and secondly, Birdcage wouldn't believe me telling the truth any quicker than me telling a big 'un. Too many times telling whoppers to him just to set him up in something was coming home to roost.

"Serves you right, Birdcage, for looking and acting so

fruity," I told him. "Now don't put that cage on till you have to."

"I guess I'll wear it when and where I want to," Birdcage pouted. Then in a lower tone as he walked away, he said, "Wear it if I want to." And with that newfound bravado, he walked down the sideline, looking back one more time at me before pulling at the sides of the helmet and spreading it gently over his now red ears. "Wear it if I want to."

Laughing, T-Bone approached me. "Don't you do that to Birdcage no more," he said, feigning concern. "That's mean, man."

"Yeah, well, he thinks I done it," I said, "and that's as good as if I had." Then I pointed out, "And did you see those big ol' ears, now red and raw?"

After a little more discussing our special moment, T-Bone and I got serious and agreed Birdcage had had enough meanness from us for one day.

A half hour later, we changed our minds. All three of us were scrimmaging—Birdcage as offensive end, and T-Bone and I playing defense. Between the two of us, we were able to yank off the helmet four more times that afternoon. His eyes got big when he saw one of us charging him with hands open and fingers extended for the capture of the Birdcage. He complained to Coach, but what could the coach really do. Since face masks were just coming out, there was no penalty invented yet for pulling the things. Still, there has to be a first time for everything.

Coach Wilkins blew his whistle, then called me and T-Bone to the sidelines. "Chief, Mull, get your asses over here." We ran over. T-Bone knew as well as I did what this meeting was going to cover. Still, we both tried to act innocent.

"Now you boys got to quit yanking Dud's silly face mask. You got me?"

"Yes sir," we said in unity.

"And just so's you'll remember," Coach said with the confidence of Solomon, "I'm charging the defense a fifteen-yard penalty just for you boys yanking Dud's helmet," adding as he pointed to Birdcage, "and setting him to squawk to me about it."

Thus it came to pass, perhaps the first penalty for yanking the face mask. It may just have been that T-Bone and I, and Birdcage in his way, were pioneers in football. There, many years ago, on a sweltering day at Lisbon Elementary School, two mean kids and a dork made history.

BLEACHERS
Chance Chambers

Sometimes "Crimson and Clover"
drops me in her room, all pink
and pillows for this county
cheerleader, smooth and long
on the bleachers with late,
blond, Barbie Benton hair.

She had the 45 with the Roulette
sticker and a suitcase turntable
as if she was going somewhere;
we only made it as far as chilled
kisses inside her father's barn
and a propane tank that we rode
like Slim Pickens loving
the bomb.

I lost her in the years
and California where she made
a living at legs contests while I spent
a piece of life on dancers with questionable
rhythm and dead-on truth.

When I found her again, she asked
"Do you miss taking chances?"
With no good answer I let the words
live and become a static loop
which drops me again
and again beneath

the bleachers where
feet-stamped thunder skies
and skirted clouds
of possibility are still
sweet, but tired
from one hundred
thousand seconds
of sweating nothing.

PARLOR COWBOYS
Susie Dunham

I was born singing headfirst into a bedpan. Not a great beginning, but I'll take it. I look at it this way—it gave me nowhere to go but up.

The house that held me as a kid sang constantly. Cowboy music, mostly. I loved cowboy music, especially when my Dad played it on his accordion. His cowboy band would come to practice in our parlor. The tiny room's wallpapered seams tugged with a drummer, a fiddler, a guitar player, and Daddy—the accordion cowboy who hummed.

I'd squeeze my pajamaed self into that room, nestle between the faded red couch and maple coffee table, and let the noise flow over me like hot fudge over vanilla ice cream. The music makers always smiled at me. Bright, wide smiles. Singing, squeezing, humming, strumming, banging, bowing. So many moving parts to watch. I was dizzy with delight.

I hummed myself to sleep with those songs. "Your Cheatin' Heart," "I Can't Help It," and "I'm Walkin' the Floor Over You."

I sang *my* favorite cowboy songs out loud, though. Songs from Hop-Along Cassidy, Gene Autry, Roy Rogers and Dale Evans.

My parents would dance in the kitchen to country and western music that floated out from the radio on top of the Fridgedaire. I wanted to join them. Become them. Singing into myself, I watched from the doorway. As they spun on the black-and-white linoleum, my mother, gleeful as she danced with my dad, smiled toward me. Other times when Dad wasn't home, she'd grab me and try to get me to jitterbug in the kitchen. My dancing was pretty much like my singing. Out of step. Out of tune.

As I grew older, I'd softly sing the songs of little girls who want to grow up, fall in love with a handsome boy, and get married. "Blue Velvet," "Soldier Boy," and eventually, "Wedding Bell Blues."

I loved music, but that love wasn't returned.

I was third clarinet, fourth seat in band. The instructor complimented me on my porcelain skin instead of my musical ability.

Chorus couldn't decide whether I was an alto or soprano. Neither could my voice.

At the prom my date spent all his time in the Boys' Room drinking with his friends. I didn't dance once. A blessing in disguise. No toes were broken that evening. Only hearts.

And in the senior play, the musical *High Button Shoes,* I sang my heart out in the chorus. Downstage.

But in the parlor with the cowboy band and the accordion cowboy who hummed, I soaked the music into my soul and my soul is always in tune.

Happy trails to me.

PERFECT LITTLE BODIES
Julia Lee Pollock

At twelve noon, Wanda watches her daughter Crystal pull out of the driveway, then peeps through a slat in the mini blinds to make sure she's gone for good. Then she goes to the freezer and pulls out a chicken and rice Lean Cuisine, peels the cardboard wrapper off, and eats it, shred by shred. Pica my ass, says Wanda, as she munches on the picture of the red pepper and water chestnuts. It's nobody's business what I eat. She tosses the frozen meal into the garbage and sits down in the middle of her white linoleum floor, scratching the dirt out of the cracks with toothpicks.

It's Wanda's day off. She works as a clerk at Belk, where she qualifies for a 25 percent discount for her daughters' clothes. They deserve the best, after all. These girls are good. Every morning they make their beds and hang up their clothes and do their chores, which consist of sweeping the kitchen floor, vacuuming the den and living room, dusting the mini blinds and the furniture, and on Fridays they clean the ceiling fans and wash the windows.

Wanda's husband Frank is also compliant. He's an Orkin man, been there sixteen years and wears a tan shirt with his name monogrammed on it. Every day, through rain, sleet, snow, and heat, he combs houses for termites and then eradicates them with drills and poison.

Wanda has been eating non-food items since giving birth to Crystal in 1983. Actually it started during her fifth month of pregnancy, when one day she was coming home from the grocery and looked over at the brown grocery bag sitting in the passenger seat and ripped off a piece and stuck it in her mouth, saturating the brown paper flat on her tongue, then chewing it up and finally swallowing it. The next week she ate a Bounty paper towel decorated with geese, and two weeks later she ate the paper wrapping off an Almond Joy. It was the paper products that appealed to her most. Once she tried to eat a tag off her new blue maternity pants and nearly choked to death.

Three o'clock rolls around, and Wanda is halfway through her secret weekly toothpick scrape when she hears Crystal pulling into the driveway. She hides the toothpicks in a drawer and turns on the TV and leaps onto the couch with a *Good Housekeeping* in her lap and a Coke and Snickers bar beside her on the glass coffee table.

Hi Mom, says Crystal, tossing her designer handbag on the kitchen table and heading straight for the fridge. What did you do today on your day off?

Went to see Aunt Pearl at the nursing home, says Wanda. After you eat those Doritos I need you to mop and wax the kitchen floor.

Crystal walks into the living room and fingers the plastic on the brass lamps from Big Lots. This plastic's tacky, she says, lifting it ever so slightly.

Leave that alone, says Wanda. Those lamp shades will get nasty if you take that plastic off. Now go clean the floor—you don't need any more of those Doritos anyway. Aren't your jeans getting a little tight?

I'm a size four, says Crystal, rolling her eyes and

slinging her wavy blond hair. Pretty high on the scale of perfection, I'd say.

Just so you'll know, I've bought you and Britney some new jeans for Christmas—fours for you and twos for her. You always have been chunkier than Britney.

Wanda then leaves the room and climbs into a hot bubble bath and sucks on the label from a bottle of Herbal Essence shampoo.

The house is one of the newest in Obion County, a $125,000 brick ranch in a new neighborhood of fifty other similar houses, garages out front. Wood floors in the living room and brown Berber carpet throughout the rest of the house. White walls, sparse pictures hung way above eye level, and a green and white rectangular rug from Wal-Mart in front of the green tweed couch and loveseat from Big Lots. The kitchen countertops are white and clean and bare, and the stovetop shines.

It's the day after Thanksgiving, and the artificial Christmas tree stands alone in the corner, adorned only with Hallmark ornaments and clear lights.

Each year the ritual is the same: Thanksgiving night at nine o'clock, Frank sets up the tree, and Wanda places each ornament in its designated spot. Underneath the tree she spreads a plain red tree skirt, and the presents are all wrapped in silver foil, separated by person. There are fifteen presents for Crystal and fifteen presents for Britney and five for Frank. The red monogrammed stockings hang from the mantel, and there is a large porcelain nativity scene placed square in the middle. Outside, clear icicle lights hang from the edge of the roof, and wreaths with copious clear lights shine from each window. The symmetrical shrubs are adorned with clear blinding lights, and out on the lawn there is a wire Santa, electrified by clearness.

Everything will be tucked back in its place the day after Christmas, precisely at five in the morning. By six o'clock, the boxes will be stacked back in the attic, and by seven o'clock, Crystal will have vacuumed all the carpets and Britney will have dusted all the furniture. Frank will have blown debris from the yard, and afterward they will eat canned Hungry Jack biscuits, pre-sliced Jimmy Dean sausage, powdered scrambled eggs, and decaffeinated coffee. It is at this moment that Wanda will experience the joy of Christmas.

Wanda soaks in Johnson's Baby Oil and shaves her pits and legs and scrapes the dead skin off her feet, exfoliates her face and body and glances at her small breasts, buoyant in the bathwater. She places a white washcloth over her pubic hair because she does not like to look at it, but she does keep the area clean—douches with Massengill every single day and uses feminine spray at every opportunity.

By the time Britney gets home, Wanda is in the kitchen fixing Hamburger Helper and iced tea and cornbread. Britney takes her laptop to her bedroom, then slips into the kitchen. Hi, Mom, she says. Need any help?

Wanda hugs her and says, Why don't you just sit down at the table and rest a minute. I'll fix you a Coke and some nachos. Do you want jalapeños and onions? You could stand a pound or two, you know.

That'd be good, says Britney, combing her fingers through her streaked blond hair and thumbing through the latest *Glamour.*

At six o'clock Frank walks through the door, goes straight to the bedroom, showers and changes into a Titans sweatshirt and new Levi's and places his work clothes in the washer and turns it on. They'll be dry by seven, and he'll iron them and hang them in his closet beside his eight other sets of work clothes. He goes into the kitchen, and Wanda fixes him a Coke and asks, How was work today?

Dirty, says Frank. Cockroaches, silverfish, termites, ladybugs. There's a plague of ladybugs this year that we can't do a thing about. Seen any 'round here?

No, says Wanda, but Ray and Carol have, down the street. And you know how they are. It's just a matter of time before they get roaches, the way they let them kids eat all over the house and throw their clothes down and stuff.

Mama wants me to come help her put up the tree, says Frank. I told her I'd be there after supper. Daddy's just too weak to help her this year.

Wanda slams the metal spatula into the sink and puts her hands on her hips. Well what's wrong with Mama that she can't do it herself? And with all their money, she could hire somebody to come and put up ten trees in that house of theirs. I need you here tonight—you'll have to call her and tell her to make other arrangements.

Frank squirms and picks up the phone. Mama, he says, I'll have to come over tomorrow night. Something's come up. No, nothing serious, nothing wrong, I just can't make it tonight. Well I'm sorry, Mama. What's he doing right now? Have you called the doctor? Okay, I'll come over there in thirty minutes and check his blood pressure.

Wanda is staring at him with laser eyes. Mama's got you wrapped around her little finger, she says. And it's always you—never Henry the wonder prick. Here she's got another grown son who never gives her the time of day, and she treats you like dog scraps. Fix your own damn supper.

Wanda backs out of the driveway in her white Taurus. Franks sits alone at the table, seeped in the story of his life, then leaves for his parents' house.

Wanda drives to Sonic and eats the little white bag from her order of fries. Things were perfect at first. Frank's parents had money and seemed generous. In 1985, Frank went to work with his daddy at the apple orchard, but things changed. Mama came to expect more and more from Frank, till his whole life was swamped in apples.

The farm showcased one of the last remaining apple orchards nestled at the edge of the broad expanse of the Mississippi flood plain, where the eroded silt hills bled into the decaying fishing hamlet of Samburg. Them Samburg people will hunt you down and throw you out there as turtle food, Mama always said, specifically to Wanda. All the difference in the world tween us and them, she'd continue. And Lake County's even worse. Old cotton, old money all over the place, nothing in the middle.

In 1988 a tornado wiped out much of the apple orchard, and Frank was rescued by the Orkin king. But oh, Frank's parents were still all right, living off their 300-plus acres and leasing out the land to soybean farmers. On the side, they bought a herd of 150 beef cattle, the perfect bait for Frank and his guilt. Mama was livid when Frank left the farm, but he and Wanda had babies to feed, and soon thereafter Wanda went to work at Belk.

Henry, the other brother, rose to high corporate ranks over in Collierville, but Mama demanded everything from Frank: loyalty, endless work, and most of all, guilt. Life became a constant yet invisible battle, for through it all Wanda wore a smile on her face at family gatherings and church and Sunday dinner at Mama's house. It was a convincing smile for years, one that served her well until Britney and Crystal got into college and the bills piled up.

Everybody else had money and freedom, and at least Frank's parents did recognize to some extent that he simply was not of great caliber and therefore they would help him more than Henry the medulla boy. Wasn't this the least they could do? Frank's parents didn't enjoy a penny of their hard-earned wealth. Why couldn't they pay for Crystal and Britney's college? Why couldn't they fork out $40,000 at Christmas to help pay for Frank's new house?

Wanda arrives back home at nine o'clock and Frank is sitting at the kitchen table. He has mopped the floor and washed down the cabinets with Murphy's Oil Soap and in Wanda's place sits a small box, wrapped in white paper with a red bow. Wanda sits and stares at the package. Open it, he says, flashing his white teeth. Wanda always did like those teeth.

Wanda opens the package and sees a diamond anniversary ring. Frank lifts it gently from the box and slips it onto her left ring finger and says, I love you, Wanda. You are the best thing that has ever happened to me. He takes her hand in his and kisses it, then leads her into the bedroom and closes the door.

Wanda likes the ring. Henry's wife will notice it, she thinks. They always come over for Christmas a week late, and Mama never says a word about it. Henry and his wife do whatever they want to do—they go to the Episcopal church, they let their kids watch *Saturday Night Live,* they gamble in Tunica and drink wine in front of their children. Elisabeth, their daughter, has a butterfly tattoo on her left ankle and a belly button ring, and is at least a size eight.

The Christmas gathering rolls around, and Henry's

wife does not notice the anniversary ring. Instead, she spends her time talking to Mama in the kitchen and picking all the cashews out of the mixed nuts. Mama seems mesmerized by this woman, somehow. Meanwhile, Wanda wears the plastered smile and helps with the dishes while Henry's wife reads a *Southern Living* cookbook. I just love these cookbooks, she says. They have the best recipes—have you tried the new Chicken Cordon Bleu? It's to die for.

Henry comes in and nuzzles the back of his wife's neck. She sure can cook, he says with a grin. Hates to clean but loves to cook, so we got a cleaning lady to come in three days a week to take care of that little problem. Then Henry pops a couple of sausage balls into his mouth and pours himself a cup of coffee. Mama, I got somebody lined up to price your timber. I'd say it's worth at least a hundred thousand.

Mama and Henry sit down at the table and seriously discuss the financial status of the farm, and Wanda's stomach nearly twists the smile off her face. Why should they get anything? They have plenty.

Henry's wife has eaten all the cashew nuts and is now devouring the peanut butter fudge. This cow's an illusion, thinks Wanda. Weighs 150 pounds and slips right into a size 6. Every part of her body is muscle and she didn't even get any stretch marks.

The annual Christmas gathering ends and everyone hugs each other with gooey smiles and says their goodbyes with Christmas loot in hand. Wanda and her family drive away to their new house across town, and Henry and his family drive back to their own nest in Collierville, eager to slip into themselves again.

What'd she say about the ring? Frank asks Wanda on the way home.

Nothing. But did you see the one on her finger? Must've been two carats.

Nah. We talked about football the whole time.

You didn't notice the ring? says Wanda. No wonder everybody's got more than us—you never pay attention to a goddamn thing.

Wanda gives Frank the silent treatment all the way home, and when they pull into their garage, Wanda grabs her salad spinner from Mama and flings it out into the yard like a Frisbee. Then she takes a drive alone and ends up at Sonic. With great defiance, Wanda eats a large order of onion rings, a number two cheeseburger, and a strawberry milkshake, and leaves all the paper wrappings inside the bag on the Sonic ledge.

For two weeks, Wanda does not shave her pits or her legs, and when she bathes, she stares at the pubic hair between her legs and shaves it into a butterfly. She cuts her hair short and hires a housekeeper and lets Crystal and Britney get tattoos and she buys them an Eminem CD that she dances to naked on her day off. She starts going to the Episcopal church and she eats cashews by the can and she buys the latest *Southern Living* cookbook.

Without question, Frank follows suit. After work he throws his clothes down on the floor and drinks beer and smokes cigarettes out on the patio with Wanda. One night he spots a cockroach on the wall above the stovetop and takes a close-up shot of it with his digital camera and has the picture enlarged, matted, and framed, and hangs it at eye level above the new brown leather sofa from Smith Home Furnishings. Crystal and Britney move out of the house and into an apartment near the University of Memphis, lunging into their sorority and out of themselves.

Mama calls Frank up one night. The cows are out, she says, and your daddy's blood pressure is up. Come over here and help me round 'em up. There's thousands of dollars over here fixin' to run away.

I'm busy, says Frank, firing up a joint while watching Wanda crawl across the floor naked to lap up milk out of a bowl like on that Madonna video.

Busy? says Mama. Well you'd better get un-busy if you ever expect a dime out of me! And your poor daddy, back there in that bed. What kind of a son are you?

Wanda looks damn good, thinks Frank as he watches her lap up the milk. Those cashews have filled her out in all the right places, and she's started shaving her legs and pits again. That short hair makes her look right feisty, too, he thinks, as he slowly hangs up the phone and unplugs it, never taking his eyes off Wanda.

He peels off his clothes and takes Wanda by the hand and leads her out under the hemlock in a corner of the fenced backyard and lays her down on the ground. The tree protects them from the howling wind, and neither of them hears Mama's car when she pulls up in the driveway, or sees her when she kicks the door after discovering it's locked, or feels her pain when she climbs back into her car and cries wee, wee, wee, all the way home.

THE GIRL WITH THE BROOM
Joyce A. O. Lee

A greasy bulb dangling on a cord from the ceiling struggled to light the dim room. It labored to spew enough light to expose the white flour that was spilled and tracked in a circle over the linoleum floor in one corner. Torn newspapers were scattered and littered the other side of the room.

Standing there in the confusion, looking around in sly amusement, the girl with the broom in her hands wrinkled her nose. She glanced down at the toddler beside her, and she understood his stern concentration. He was quite still and straining, and immediately, she recognized the source of the foul odor filling the kitchen.

"Davey! Jesus!" she exclaimed.

The other child, a rowdy four-year-old, looked up and giggled, then continued with his handiwork. He was purposely shredding the papers into bits and sprinkling them on the floor, making more work for her.

Exasperated, she let the little one finish his business. Then she picked him up, slinging him over her hip with his offensive backside as far from her front as she could manage.

"Come on, Danny," she said to the older boy. "You two are going upstairs."

"I don't want to," Danny answered stubbornly, like a

child accustomed to having his own way. He stuck out his lower lip and opened his hands, allowing many more shreds of paper to cast off across the floor.

The girl drew a deep breath and instantly regretted it.

"Don't argue with me!" she scolded. "Davey's filled his pants."

After all, he wasn't her kid. His mother could clean him up. She put her free hand on the back of the older boy and pushed him forward. He balked a little, but he knew she was firm, and he gave up.

As the three crowded noisily up the narrow wood stairs, a door opened, and light appeared at the top. Materializing as a dark silhouette, her father was standing there.

"Davey's filled his pants," she explained, and handed over the boy.

Her father took the child and placed him gingerly on the floor, and Danny and Davey disappeared down the dimly lit hall. She could hear the patter of their feet crossing the upstairs floor.

Passing on the unpleasant task, her father replied, "Danielle can take care of him."

The man at the top of the stairs wore his Levi's tight. He was bare to the waist, and in the shadowy reflection of the dusky light, the girl could sense the rippling strength of his biceps, hardened by physical labor. Her father was a handsome man with dark, compelling eyes, an enticing smile, and a tempting body to match.

The girl had a chuckle to herself. No wonder Danielle was so jealous and bottled a gamey temper, as well.

A clap of thunder rattled the old house. All day, rain had threatened, and now, adding to the fervor, it was here.

"Did you get that mess cleaned up?" her father asked.

"No, not yet."

"Well, get it done and go on to bed."

"Why don't you come down here with me?"

She knew, in her own time, she could work on him.

"No," he answered.

"Please."

His mouth twisted in a roguish smile. An entertaining thought had crossed his mind.

"I said no, girl, not tonight. Now do what you've been told."

With her pleading silenced, the girl turned and went back down the stairs. At least her place to sleep was comfortable and in front of the fireplace where it would be warm and bright all night. She'd add another log for safe measure.

As she entered the parlor, his face appeared, startled, like the flash of lightning through the window. He'd been there in the rain watching for her. She crossed to the door and let him inside.

Back in the kitchen, the floor was a mess. Papers and powdery footprints in a morass were all over the place. Well, she'd finish it later, or in the morning, or not at all. It wasn't her mess or her temper that caused it. Let Danielle do it.

The girl pulled a chair close under the light. She stood on it and carefully turned the hot bulb until it was extinguished. Stepping down, she felt her way in the pulse of the lightning, back across the room, down the hall, and into the firelight.

Already, the face from the window had found his way inside and was sprawled the full length of the couch. The girl knelt on the floor beside him and pulled the wet shirt over his head.

Laying her body over him, she began to kiss his chest for a taste of the damp, salty skin. Her fingers twisted and toyed with the coiled hairs growing there. In time, her hand slipped down his leg, seeking his thigh, and he moaned when she gripped him and waited.

"Oh, Missy," the man whispered through her soft hair and into her ear. "What have you done to me?"

MISS OCTOBER
Chance Chambers

"Did you know neon buzzes?"

Nova stood in the doorway, waiting for Leonard to say something. When he didn't, she let herself in and dropped on the bed.

"Once, when I was real gone in this little grease bucket just east of Humboldt, I leaned against a window with a glowing beer sign." Nova bunched a pillow up against the side of her face. "I heard it like I never had before, like a bee just inside my ear. Almost tickled."

Leonard thought to himself that some of Nova's real gone insights were more than many clear-minded people get in a lifetime. Turning to close the door, he noticed the neon sign by the highway.

"I've never heard it."

He walked to the bathroom to wash his hands. With the water running, Leonard looked in the mirror. Gray was starting to speckle his nearly black hair. He tried to remember his last haircut. His cheeks looked slimmer than last week, he thought. Before turning off the water, he traced the scars and scabs on his face. Then he washed his hands again.

Nova was asleep when Leonard came out of the bathroom. He turned off the television and walked outside into the parking lot. Across it he could see the highway settling down for the night. Looking at the asphalt, even when there was no traffic, made him feel the world was still spinning.

Behind him, time had been snagged on the points of fifteen cone-shaped hotel rooms. Caught was 1937, the year a white man had an epiphany from visiting a Sioux reservation and an upside down ice cream cone restaurant. Inspired, he set concrete to grass and stucco to concrete and covered it in magic white paint that almost glowed at dusk. When he was finished, he christened his work Wigwam Village and plugged in the neon signs. SLEEP IN A WIGWAM. VACANCY.

For years to come, families, salesmen, and lone travelers with empty eyes would all beat a moth's path to the illuminated gas in glass. Once inside their tranquil teepees, they would bounce and sleep on log beds or toss briefcases on wicker chairs. Or they would sit at the matching writing desk with a mirror, pull a Bible from the drawer, and read Revelation by the table's little lamp until they couldn't sleep.

Leonard had seen brochures for Wigwam Village at rest stops all his life, so when his headlights hit the big Office Wigwam one night, he knew the hotel right away. And he knew he couldn't pass it.

He took another look at the highway, then walked back to Wigwam Number Fifteen. Nova was still asleep. He closed the door and checked the lock, turning the knob one, two, three, four times.

"Caught you." A whisper came from the bed.

"Caught me what?"

"Caught you counting." Nova raised her head a little.

"You were dreaming."

Nova smiled and turned over. Her sleeve had nudged

up, and Leonard could see the needle marks. Almost unconsciously, he counted them; there were new ones.

"Caught me." Nova's tone was less playful now.

"I didn't mean to stare." Leonard looked down. "Sorry."

Nova sighed. "Why are you always apologizing?" She shook her head and leaned up on an elbow. "You never really do anything to be sorry for."

"I'm sure I do."

"Look around you. Look at me. You're a saint."

"I'm afraid of what I might do." Leonard squirmed a little.

"What do you mean?"

Leonard hesitated. "Sometimes I have these flashes . . . these thoughts that hit me. They are so vivid."

"What kind of thoughts?"

Leonard looked at his hands. "Things I don't want to talk about, things you don't want to hear. Violent thoughts. Mostly about hurting people." He looked up with an expression that seemed to say, "Okay, you can run now." When he saw that Nova was going to stay and listen, he continued.

"Then I imagine going through with those things. Kind of test myself. That just makes it worse."

Nova sat up and studied Leonard for a moment. "Look, I've known you for almost two months now. I come in here every night; I sit on your bed for hours. Tonight, I fell asleep. What did you do? You stood in the parking lot, then jiggled the doorknob an even number of times. I think you can take it easy. Those are just thoughts."

"Sometimes they seem so real, it feels like I could go through with them."

"But they're not real and you haven't." Nova pushed the last word, hoping it would stick.

A look of exaggerated enlightenment fell over Leonard's face and he said, "Oh, okay. Thanks, I get it now."

Nova tossed a pillow at him and grinned. Suddenly she looked pale. "I need to go."

"Nova—"

"Don't start!" Nova snapped. "We've gone over this." She held out her arm. "You think that looks bad, you should take a look at your face! Scratch, scratch." She clawed at the air.

Leonard opened the door and motioned her out.

"I, I didn't mean that. You know how I get."

"I know." Leonard relaxed a little. "It's okay."

Nova bumped Leonard as she walked past.

"Sorry." Leonard moved to the side.

Nova looked down, then at Leonard's face. "And you apologize." Glancing at her hands, she asked, "Have you ever imagined hurting me?"

Leonard fidgeted; he didn't want to answer.

"Leonard?"

Finally he whispered, "Yes."

Nova walked back inside and hopped on the bed. "Come here."

"What?" Leonard asked.

"Come here and lay beside me."

Leonard walked over and eased down next to Nova. His elbows and shoulders were stiff as he tried to leave at least two inches between their arms. Nova noticed him trying not to look at the scissors on the table next to the bed. She reached over him and pulled them across the table until they were less than an inch from his arm. Nova then put her head on his shoulder. Leonard was rigid at first, but finally slid his arm behind Nova and put his hand on her hair.

Nova fell asleep first. Her body was small and light against Leonard. The feel of it betrayed her presence when awake and chattering. He looked down at her, truly noticing her physically for maybe the first time. Nova wore no makeup. Leonard tried to imagine her with lipstick; he couldn't. Her lips were narrow, but the top one curled out a little, feigning fullness. A dirty blond strand of hair had covered her eye. Leonard brushed it back and listened to her breath until he heard the faint sound of a concertina.

That was Mr. Wink, the hotel owner, in the Office Wigwam. Every night about this time he played through his Civil War repertoire that made him a favorite at reenactments in three counties. Now Leonard could hear the tambourine and harmonica. He smiled when he thought of Mr. Wink playing the tambourine with his foot. Leonard's eyes started to close. Just as he heard Mr. Wink's nasal tenor cut through the wheezing of the concertina, he fell asleep.

Sometime during the night, Leonard thought he sat up and looked out the tiny window next to the headboard of his bed to see the grass slowly darken in the moonlight. It must be blood from the soldiers in Mr. Wink's songs, he thought.

Mr. Wink played until almost two o'clock in the morning. He played later when his only guests were Gold Star Customers. That's what he called extended stay guests. Gold Star Customers paid what they could, if they could, and were usually more nocturnal than weekenders or one-nighters. Nova reached Gold Star status around the fall of the Berlin Wall. She was Mr. Wink's only Cold War Gold Star customer.

The next morning, Nova woke up first. She and Leonard were still dressed and had barely moved during the night. She climbed over Leonard to look out the tiny window behind the bed.

"Leonard! Leonard, wake up! It's beautiful!"

Sometime in the early hours, the trees behind Wigwam Number Fifteen had dropped their leaves, covering the clearing below with gold, red, and brown.

Leonard rolled over and squinted through the curtains. No part of the ground could be seen for a fresh, ankle-high layer of leaves. Among the trees was a scattering of discarded tables, mirrors, and other replaced hotel furnishings. In the middle of the clearing was an old radiator heater that sprouted from the ground like some strange and coiled metal plant.

Leonard stood up and looked out again. Nova was already opening the door.

Suddenly something flew past the window and scattered the leaves with an impact. Nova jumped up out of the settling leaves and laughed, motioning for Leonard to join her. He started toward the door, and then looked back at the table where the scissors had been. They were exactly where Nova left them. He ran outside.

Just as Leonard reached Nova, she jumped toward him and catapulted as many leaves as she could with her arms. He ran after her, and she ducked behind a tree. They both laughed and chased each other around the clearing with arms full of brittle, red, and gold flames. The ground crunched wherever they stepped.

Stirred by the commotion, Mr. Wink walked out of the Office Wigwam dressed like a Gettysburg foot soldier. Jagged new colors swallowed his boots as he smiled at

Nova and Leonard chasing each other. After finding a stump, he sat down, opened his bag, and covered himself in a tin and reed orchestra. With a slight sway, he began to push and pull his concertina, stomp and lift the tambourine. Melodies about cannon fire and river retreats mixed with laughter, stirring a breeze across the Village. One by one, other doors opened and out walked Gold Star Customers.

There was the highway preacher with a green bus. He had blessed the Village, one wigwam at a time. The writer in Wigwam Number Thirteen came out. She almost never did, spending her time trying to feel the couple that had died there on their honeymoon twenty years ago. Even the man who never spoke, but only stared at the sky all night in front of Wigwam Number Seven wandered out.

Everyone started throwing leaves and dancing to upbeat songs about bullet wounds and sweethearts left behind. The morning thickened with chatter and the calliope breaths of Mr. Wink's harmonica and concertina. "Ching ching chi-ching," the foot tambourine kept time. Between songs, Mr. Wink drank from a canteen.

Nova and Leonard rolled in leaves, danced, and chased each other a dozen times. Out of breath they collapsed in a deep crackling drift against a tree. Nova burrowed underneath, and Leonard followed playfully. They burst headfirst from the pile, spitting and flinging leaves. Leonard moved back and reclined against the tree; Nova slid back and rested on his chest and stomach. Both were still shoulder-deep in the drift.

A few feet across from them, a broken mirror from one of the wigwams leaned against another tree. Nova and Leonard looked at themselves in the cracked glass, noticing how the leaves had fallen on them. Suddenly, Leonard's arms pushed through the foliage to wrap around Nova, so that they looked like they were her arms.

They laughed as Leonard's hands and arms and Nova's face moved in exaggerated glamour poses.

After a while, Nova's face grew serious; her eyes seemed to see deeper into the mirror.

"Look at us," she said. "No marks."

Leonard leaned his head to look around Nova's. He watched as his smooth arms moved slowly now with her clear face. "Smooth as a magazine."

"Yeah, just like in a magazine," Nova whispered. "Like Miss October."

Nova and Leonard stopped posing as a leaf fell from Nova's hair, tumbling alongside her soft, wind-chilled face to land on Leonard's arm, unmarked and nearly hairless. Nova leaned back against Leonard, took a deep breath, and smiled with her head turned enough for Leonard to see. She closed her eyes and soon she was asleep.

When Nova opened her eyes, Leonard had gone. She had fallen back and was nestled in a dark, brittle mattress. The village was very quiet. The party must be over, she thought.

Nova stood up and looked around. She didn't see anyone. She walked around the village, and no one was there. Even Mr. Wink's Office Wigwam was empty. No sounds of televisions or radios in the wigwams. No cars in the half-moon parking lot.

Nova started down the highway. She walked around the bend just past the village and found a service station. At the edge of the parking lot, someone in a giant polar bear suit was walking back and forth, trying to sell gas, ice cream, or something. She wasn't sure. The bear waved at the occasional passing car with one hand and held his head on with the other.

Nova walked up and asked, "Did anyone from the hotel come by here? A man with a concertina? Another with a scarred face? Did you see a green bus?"

The bear shrugged and danced a half jig. Then it walked away, turning and motioning for Nova to follow. So she did.

The bear led Nova to the men's restroom in back of the service station. Nova stopped and shook her head. The bear waved playfully and went inside. Nova hesitated, and then followed. The little room was cramped; the door swung closed anyway.

Nova thought she heard music in the distance, but she wasn't sure. The bear reached behind the toilet and pulled out a bag. From it, he took a syringe and tourniquet and offered them to Nova. She hesitated, but not much.

She tied the tourniquet and found the vein. The music was louder now. When she was finished, she noticed the bear was pushing his giant white pants down around his padded fabric feet. When he bent over, Nova saw her face in the mirror over the sink. But it was the face of a younger Nova, a teenager, not more than sixteen. Now she could tell the music was from a concertina.

"Nova, Nova."

Someone was shaking Nova. She awoke and looked around. It was Leonard; she was still with him in the leaves. A parade led by Mr. Wink and his concertina made its way between the mirror and Nova and Leonard.

"You started struggling in your sleep." Leonard's mouth was next to Nova's ear. "Must have been some dream."

Nova leaned forward. "Just about my sixteenth birthday party."

Suddenly Nova and Leonard were lifted off the ground by hands from Mr. Wink's parade. They marched around to the parking lot in front of the Village. It was early dusk, and the wigwams had their faint glow. Everyone danced to Mr. Wink's music, partners were changed and changed again, and no one thought of anything else.

Leonard was trying to play Mr. Wink's harmonica when he realized he hadn't seen Nova for a while. He looked toward her wigwam; the door was open. He started toward her room, but heard someone shout, "Nova, no!"

He turned around to see Nova almost at the top of the hotel sign where the neon words had just become luminous in the dusk. She was naked and climbing slowly. When her head reached the red glowing SLEEP almost at the top, she craned her neck around and shouted, "Leonard! It's buzzing!"

"Nova, please!" Leonard shouted.

"Leonard! Leonard, you know what I'm gonna do for you? I'm gonna give you a pretend crucifixion for your imagined sins!"

Nova clumsily turned herself around, pivoting her feet on the narrow bar running between two rods that supported the sign. VACANCY in incandescent white letters was at her feet.

Leonard ran toward the sign.

When Nova had her heels on the bar, she lifted one hand from a rod she had been using to steady herself and stretched it out across the sign. With her back against the words IN A, she clutched the A of WIGWAM.

"Nova, don't!" Leonard was almost to the sign.

Nova released the second rod to reach across to the other side. For almost a second, she looked graceful, floating. The flat teepee-shaped top of the sign above her transformed Nova into a Las Vegas dancer with some oversized headdress. Suspended in the air, she was unfettered and more tranquil than ever. Her hand grasped the neon W now all the way to her right. The glass tube couldn't support her weight; it broke from the sign.

"Nova!"

Nova lost her footing and fell to the concrete just before Leonard could reach the sign. She landed face down.

Leonard kneeled next to Nova and lowered his ear to her mouth. From there, he could hear the complete silence of the parking lot. No laughing, no chatter, no concertina. No breath.

By the time the ambulance arrived, the parking lot was completely dark except for the neon SLEEP IN A _IGWAM. Leonard sat on the asphalt underneath the buzzing letters. The ambulance left in no real hurry, and Leonard fell asleep with his back against the sign.

The next day, the Village was quiet. Around one o'clock, Leonard packed and left his room. He didn't bother to close the door, letting it swing with the breeze. He walked to the Office Wigwam and checked out. Mr. Wink gave him a nod as he hung up the key to Wigwam Number Fifteen.

Leonard tossed his bags in the trunk of his car without a second glance, pulled out of the parking lot, and steered around the bend just beyond the Village. There he passed a service station where a giant polar bear walked back and forth, trying to sell gas, ice cream, or something. He wasn't sure.

ASTRONOMY, LAYMAN STYLE
Nelda Rachels

Always on the lookout for the perfect educational experience, my husband and I couldn't wait to introduce
our children to their very first lunar eclipse. On the
scheduled night, with lawn chairs, blankets, pillows, tape
measure, flashlight, binoculars, mosquito repellent, hoe
(for the odd snake), and two children in tow, we installed
ourselves in the backyard under a sky where the moon and
the neon glow of stars took center stage.

We vied for the best seats. My husband's tape measure
came in handy for this bit of "family planning." We spaced
the children at least twenty-four inches apart so no one's
elbow or toe touched anyone else's elbow or toe. After we
had at last settled in (with blankets and pillows divided—
equally, of course), we lapsed into a reverent and blissful
silence—for about two seconds.

Then it was that the older child, our daughter, who
was just entering puberty and therefore excused from any
mysterious or irrational behaviors, began humming the
latest rock tune while meowing at the cats, which had
decided to join the lunar watch.

The tune was not to my liking, nor the meowing, so I
requested she stop so the rest of us could concentrate.

"Concentrate? On an eclipse? But whatever for?" she

asked, incredulous.

I gushed, "So we can meditate, be at one with the universe, admire God's handiwork, and watch this once-in-a-blue-moon eclipse. Besides, the noise is getting on my nerves."

"What's an eclipse?" asked our younger, usually happier, but sometimes confused son.

My husband sighed. We had, of course, previously explained it all with our ancient 1973 encyclopedia and textbooks, but he tried again, this time more creatively. "It's when the moon, the sun, and the earth stand in a straight line up in the sky—for what, who knows? Maybe they're in the army. At any rate, the earth butts between the sun and the moon. The earth, bully that he is, glowers darkly over the moon, but eventually the line breaks up and the moon shines again. All's well that ends well, hey?"

Not to be outdone, I added, "It's as if the moon plays peek-a-boo with the earth while they're standing in the army chow-line. It's simple, really."

Our daughter shook her head and groaned.

Two more seconds of quiet. The dogs joined us, scratching fleas.

"Ugh! The dogs stink!" shouted our son.

"So?" retorted our daughter. "So do your feet!"

"Do not!"

"Do too!"

"Do not!"

"Stop it, you two! What happened to meditation?" I asked.

After more silence, just long enough for the heavy black curtain filled with planets and stars to begin its descent on our consciousness, our son asked, "Uh, what is that round thing? The earth?"

We groaned.

"Earth to Bro, Earth to Bro, come back to Earth, Bro!"

"So? You're from Mars!" Sticking out his tongue, he taunted in his most singsongy voice, "Sis looks like a Martian, Sis looks like a Martian!"

"Do not!"

"Do too!"

"Do not!"

"Stop! Quiet, please," I begged.

After two quiet seconds, Sis complained, "I'm cold. I need a sweater."

"Me too!"

After the children left, my husband said, "I bet they really went in to get some of those cookies you baked this afternoon."

A female voice shouted, "Don't get too many, or I'm telling!"

I felt my husband's smile in the darkness. "Didn't I tell you?"

The children came back, giggling, minus the sweaters. They decided to ignore our carefully measured seating arrangements and share a lawn chair. Bro pulled the dog's tail. Sis bumped Bro, but before a fight could break out, we all saw it—a streak of light across the sky, as if a tube of a neon light had just flickered on, then off.

"It's a shooting star," I decreed.

"It's a lightning bug! A plane!" The children chimed.

My husband started, "No, it's—"

"Superman!" we shouted in unison.

We laughed, and then grew silent.

Two seconds later, someone called for the binoculars.

"It's my turn!"

"No, it's my turn!"

"I brought them out here!"

Our son got another turn, a long one, in which he zoned out in a trance. Finally, he lowered the binoculars and blurted, "What is that round thing, again?"

We groaned.

"Oh, I remember, it's the moon getting hidded from the sun."

"Thank you for remembering!" Sis exclaimed.

"So? I don't want to be an as-tro-whatever, anyway."

Our daughter corrected, "Astronaut. You don't want to be an astronaut. Good thing! You'd land your rocket on the wrong planet!"

"Would not!"

"Would too!"

"Would not!"

Two seconds of silence later, we began drifting, one by one, back into the house. The eclipse was taking too long. Only my husband stayed to watch.

I asked him the next day, "So, how was the eclipse?"

He answered sheepishly, "I fell asleep."

I laughed. "You know, I think our family just set astronomy back two hundred years."

"Oh, further than that," he insisted. "We pushed it back into the Pre-Copernican Era, at least!"

VANILLA
Jennifer Dix

I am pale, a creamy vanilla, soft and subdued.

On the farm I am the color of dried cornhusks,
wheat in the fields and Mama's buttermilk biscuits.

During the holidays I am Aunt Myra's banana pudding
and the eggnog spiked with a touch of Jack Daniel's.

Before you were born I was the rich velvety color of
freshly churned butter and the pile of newly shorn
lamb's wool waiting to be spun.

In the home I am the vanilla candle you bought at
Wal-Mart, your grandmother's hand lotion and the
gallon bucket of ice cream in your freezer.

At the office I am manila file folders, computer
monitors, Post-It notes and letterhead.

A rich downy pastel, I shine in pale moonlight and
stain buttercups, roses, and ivory wedding dresses.

I am versatile enough to go with the vibrant red scarf
or shiny black dancing shoes and comfortable enough
to go to the party alone.

Pleasant to the eyes and soft to the touch
I make no apologies for blending in.

I am feminine, yet strong, subtle and easygoing.

Confident but not arrogant, I complement everyone
and overpower none.

MILE MARKER 15
C. K. Speroff

Alex and I pull up past the milepost onto a gravel
shoulder of the road and stop. I check the dashboard
clock. It's 2:30 p.m. We are right on time, and apparently,
the first to arrive. It's an ordinary intersection on a two-
lane country road. "Mile Marker 15," I say in a singsong
voice, reassuring myself we are at the right spot.
Reassuring myself we are doing the right thing.

Black-faced sheep graze in the pasture on the other
side of a taut barbed wire fence. Ramshackle, tin-roofed
sheds sit sporadically about the farm. A white house sits at
one corner of the field, a gravel drive leading up to its
untidy yard. A stand of wild olive trees on the other side
of the road separates us from full view of an old barn and
its fading white steeple. In the distance the Sawtooth
Mountains, still capped with snow, rise to greet us.

Alex snaps some Nirvana into the tape deck. I turn
the volume down.

"Hey!" he yells.

"Can't we just listen to the quiet for a little while?"

"No way," he says and turns the volume back up to full
blast. He leans back and shuts his eyes.

"Well, put your earphones on, then!"

He complies with a shrug, the tension conveyed in

harsh words and tones of voice suspending into hushed, invisible tightropes between us. Silence manifests its cloak on each of us, concealing tender, festering wounds. I close my eyes and, except for the chafing songs of summer crickets and the grating of sheep chewing grass and thistle, I hear nothing but a silent roar. How is it possible to feel such torment in the midst of all this tranquility?

The sun begins to burn my skin through the open window. Eventually, I slide out and walk around to the shaded side of the van. More out of habit than anything, I search for rocks with interesting shapes and hues. A Great Pyrenees eyes me as I approach the fence and barks a warning from the field of sheep he is guarding. There is a boundary here, and I am at its edge.

Some large, smooth stones lie among the foxtails, which have grown up through the gravel. I turn a white one over with my foot and pick it up. The stone is warm, and I press it between my hands. I hold it out to Alex, and he lifts the right earphone from his long, curly hair, raising a dark eyebrow.

"Want a hot rock?" I ask.

"Nope." He puts the earphone back in place and closes his eyes. I hold onto the warmth of the stone a few more seconds and then place it in the pocket of the black windbreaker I often wear to soften the push of the Idaho winds.

The jacket is faded now, its pockets once bulging treasure chests from the hikes Alex and I used to take together since before he could walk. In the beginning I fastened him into the carrier, hoisted him on my back, and did his hiking for him. As he got older and his curiosity grew, our hikes took on a hunter/gatherer mentality. We searched for anything nature had offered up to us. Snails, blue jay feathers, fallen bird nests, and moss from river paths. Dead starfish, crab legs, and shells from coastal shorelines. Rocks from mountain fields, geodes from the desert. These pockets have been empty for some time now, frayed and full of holes, but strong enough yet to cradle the weight of this one last treasure.

"They're fifteen minutes late, Mom," Alex says, taking off his headphones. "Let's go."

"They'll be here soon enough. Look at the directions again and see if we're at the right spot."

Alex picks up the small yellow note off the dashboard and reads it. "Yeah, this has to be it," he says, dropping the note on the floorboard. I slip behind the steering wheel once more. Alex leans back into his headrest. "It doesn't make sense, being picked up in the middle of nowhere like this. It's gotta be some kinda cult."

"I promise you, it isn't."

"It's probably a scam, then," he says. "We send them all the money, we wait for them out here in no-man's land, and they never show."

"You did read the letter, Alex. They warned us that some of the other kids might experience delays at the airports. We'll just have to wait."

Thirty minutes pass by. "Let's go, Mom. They don't expect us to be dumb enough to wait this long," he says.

I want to scream at him that if it weren't for his own stupidity, if he and his buddies hadn't been partying it up in an empty house on Halloween with that damned headbanger crap he calls music blaring through the walls and all the windows lit up for the neighbors to see, we wouldn't be stuck in this hellhole in the middle of Idaho. But I restrain myself. Maybe I *should* scream. How could he have been so careless?

Self-doubt and panic, by now old familiar feelings, begin to take hold. They turn their gnarled fingers and point blame in my direction. What about *you*? Have *you* been careless with your son's young life?

It won't be long now. A busload of troubled kids will pull up at Mile Marker 15. Alex will join them. He'll go to survival camp with them. They're all substance abusers and hell-raisers in general. They're referred to as youth at risk by society.

"Youth at risk? That's so lame!" Alex remarked one day while browsing through the information pamphlets. "Why don't they just call us fucked-up teenagers?"

Twenty-one days is what it will take, they say. There is a wrenching pain in my gut. Maybe this is a mistake. Is Alex going to die out there? What will he eat and drink? How will he stay warm at night? There are rattlesnakes out there. I die a little on the inside with each tormenting thought.

I am ready to burst from the iced tea I drank on the way out here. So is Alex. "I've gotta take a piss," he says and gets out of the car. As he urinates on Mile Marker 15, I look the other way. An elderly couple in a large sedan pass by slowly. They glare at Alex and then at me and turn their faces swiftly away to the road ahead in stiff-necked arrogance.

Two boys from the sheep ranch hop on their bikes and pedal past our van, stop, and turn around. "We were wonderin' if you need any help," they ask.

"No," I say. "We're waiting for someone. They were supposed to be here an hour ago. I hope we're not bothering you."

"No, ma'am. We were just wonderin' is all. Would you like a cold drink?"

"No, thanks. We're okay."

"Yes, ma'am." The boys head back. I see kitchen curtains at the farmhouse fall back into place. Their mother, most likely. Bet she's wondering what we're doing parked alongside their pasture all this time.

"I'm hungry, Mom," Alex says.

"Oh, I suppose it wouldn't hurt to give you one last good meal, and I need to find a restroom, anyway. But leave a note in case they come before we get back."

Alex eagerly scribbles a note on a piece of sticky-back paper: It's 4:00. We've gone back to Gooding to use the john and get some grub. Back in a minute. —Alex P.

Sticking it to the mile marker post, he says, "Let's go, Mom. Hurry up."

I make a U-turn and head back to town. Worried the wind will blow our note away, worried we'll miss the bus, I press down hard on the accelerator. Close to Gooding, a Pizza Hut comes into view.

"There, Mom. Stop there!"

"Alex, we don't have time to wait for pizza."

"Well, then, Dairy Queen," he says. "A Circle K—anything!"

Is Alex going to starve to death out there? I am desperate for a restroom, but just as I'm about to pull into the Dairy Queen, a bus the color of pea soup drives past.

"What an ugly color," I say, and then chastise myself. How can I be shallow at a time like this?

Staring out of one of the bus windows is a small, adolescent boy wearing a pair of fluorescent green sunglasses, a part of snowboarding gear I have come to know quite well since moving to Idaho three years ago. I glance at the pair Alex is wearing today, nearly identical to the boy's on the bus, except Alex's is in a striking hue of shimmering yellow.

I recall Alex's snowboarding excursions the last three winters up to Bogus Basin with his friends in a school bus, escorted only by the driver. Every Saturday morning before dawn, if the roads were passable, they'd go. It was a two-hour drive from the truck stop outside of town. On the mountain, an occasional avalanche sweeps over the narrow road leading to the ski lodge, stranding any motorists in its path. Sometimes the roads become icy or blizzards render them too dangerous. During the past three years, I have worried about Alex's safety on those ski trips, but how was I to know the most pressing danger lay in what transpired within, and not outside the ski bus?

It seemed like such a wholesome way for a kid to spend his time. All that mountain air and vigorous exercise with a group of friends. It seemed safe until Anne, another mother, called me saying she had found a paper bag of mushrooms buried deep inside her son's backpack after his return from a ski trip.

Too naïve to know what a bag of mushrooms could possibly mean other than simply an unusual snack for a boy of fifteen, I said, "Hmm. Alex usually takes Doritos and Coke." Of course, somewhere beneath my subconscious level, I knew what those mushrooms were about; the truth of it just hadn't occurred to me until Anne began spelling it out. As soon as Alex was in the shower that evening, I committed the dirty deed of rifling through his backpack, finding nothing, feeling unforgivably reprehensible.

"All clear at our house," I told Anne after calling her back. I felt relieved. I felt righteous.

"Justin's mother mentioned something about a bag of mushrooms in his backpack today," I said to Alex later that night.

"What?" Alex frowned.

"Mushrooms . . . in Justin's backpack after the ski trip today. She said she didn't put any in his lunch."

"I didn't see him eating any mushrooms. But he does eat pretty weird shit sometimes."

"I don't think Justin's mother was referring to snacks. I think she was referring to drugs. Do you know about magic mushrooms?"

"What? Justin's mom is crazy!"

"Alex, I need to know what this is about. I need to know what you know about this and whether you are or are not experimenting with drugs."

"Mom, I would never do anything that stupid. How can you even ask me that? It's insulting! Just don't talk to Justin's mom anymore. That woman is a lunatic!"

I wanted to believe him. I wanted to believe that my son was experiencing his youth unharmed and untainted. I did believe him for a while, until I smelled an unmistakable odor seeping beneath his bedroom door.

"How do *you* know what pot smells like?" he asked in an accusing tone after I confronted him.

"I've been around it, Alex. I know."

"Yeah, well, I don't know what you're smelling, but it's not pot."

Alex slammed his door and turned up the volume of his CD player. Death metal music is what he called it. Sounded like death to me, all right, the voice of old

Beelzebub himself, from the deepest ring of hell. Like eerie chanting in the background of a terror movie, it frightened me, filled me with dread. I was angry that it was in my house, infiltrating Alex's mind and maybe his very soul. Only once did I express my alarm upon hearing the god-awful sound of it.

"You have to listen to the lyrics to understand it, Mom. You don't get it, so shut the hell up about it," Alex said.

I began to search his room and backpack after every ski trip or any overnighter with his friends. The most I ever found were cigarettes and lighters, even empty beer cans hidden in the back of his closet. I could accept the cigarettes and beer, as bad as they were, but not drugs. Not Alex. And even though I saw the evidence in his face—the runny nose, his sleepy bloodshot eyes, his lethargy, the more than usual cravings for junk food—I still could not believe it.

His personality changed, too. He refused to join us at the dinner table, taking his meals to his room and locking the door. He rarely spoke to us, and when he did, it was with insults.

"Why don't you sit at the table with us?" his dad or I asked at nearly every meal. But he did not respond, and we chose to let it go.

Alex took little interest in school, just barely getting by. One day the principal called to say that he had been caught smoking pot behind a school building with another boy. And not long after that, the police caught him drinking at a school football game. He was suspended for all of this, and we reluctantly made arrangements to have him tested regularly.

"I'm telling you now, they're not gonna find anything in my urine, so it's just a waste of my time and your money."

Sure enough, Alex was right. Nothing showed up. But I learned by Alex's own admittance that there are ways to get around the urine test and that any kid who knew anything, knew exactly what to do, which is what Alex was doing all along. If he hadn't got caught at that one party, he might have gotten away with everything.

On Halloween, Alex and a few of his friends were arrested for breaking and entering and possession of illegal substances and underage drinking. One of the boys ran away. Another was sleeping on the back porch. Another hid successfully underneath a pile of liquor boxes in the basement. The rest of them were thrown to the ground, roughed up, and handcuffed.

Later, in juvenile court we were given the choice of either sending Alex to the juvenile delinquent center or to a survival camp for teenagers. We chose the camp, hoping it would have a positive effect. I wanted the old Alex back, not this alien form of what was once my son. I could take losing everything, anything except the loss of my child.

I knocked on his door that Halloween night after we brought him home from the police station, wanting to talk, wanting to get him to talk. Tell me, Alex. Please. Why are you doing this to yourself? What have we done to you? What have I done? But when Alex opened his bedroom door, all I could do was weep. I could not speak a single word . . . only his name. "Alex."

Alex put his arms around me and held me. "It's okay, Mom. Don't cry. Everything will be okay. Don't worry about me. I can handle it." It was a tender moment that I will never forget, but I wasn't sure if it was Alex or the drugs talking. Still, I knew he was there underneath it all—somewhere.

"There's the bus!" I announce, as I search for a spot in the road to turn around.

"That's not them, Mom." Alex says.

"I'm afraid it is," I reply. My stomach stands on its head.

"Aww. We can at least get a Coke, can't we?"

"Sorry. You had your last good meal at lunch today."

"Mom, I want some food," Alex whines.

"I'm sure they'll feed you tonight."

Like a madwoman, I make a swift U-turn and speed back toward Mile Marker 15, passing all vehicles in my way. My heart is pounding a hole in my chest.

"What if they don't wait for us?" I say.

"They'll wait, Mom."

Alex groans in his seat, as I strain to catch a glimpse of the pea-green bus ahead of us. Am I really this anxious to be rid of my son? I glance over at him. The tears come quickly now. I want them to take him.

Back at the meeting spot, the bus is waiting. I park behind it and another bus pulls up behind me. "It's the same damn color as the first bus," I say, as I look in the rearview mirror.

"What?" says Alex, jerking his head around.

"Oh nothing, Alex. It just seems like they could come up with a cheerier color than slime green for their buses." The color reminds me of the walls of a state hospital where I once worked as a medical transcriptionist.

"Mom, you're so weird. What do you think this is, Kiddy Camp?" With those parting words, Alex steps out of our van.

A young man standing by the first bus introduces himself to Alex, shaking his hand. A woman walks up and greets me.

"Mrs. Parker?"

"Yes, that's me," I confess, stepping out of my van. Guilt cuts through my mothering heart, making mincemeat of what little bits of pride still remain, so that there is nothing left, nothing but desperation.

"I'm Mandy Bradley, one of the counselors. I want to assure you that Alex will be just fine and that he's in safe hands."

"Oh. Thank you," I reply like a stupid little mouse.

"And you can call anytime to check on his progress."

"Okay, I will, thanks."

"Thank you for trusting us with your son."

Trust you with my son? I can't trust my own parenting skills, let alone the guidance skills of a stranger at a juvenile boot camp.

As we shake hands, I notice the well-defined muscles on her lean arms, her long, graying hair, and warm manner. Like the rest of them, she is youthful and fit. I'm wearing makeup today. I was going for that she's-got-it-together look. Now I realize these gung-ho survivalist types are not fooled by my outward appearance, and standing among them, I feel strangely reassured.

Before I know it, Alex is seated in the bus. Another counselor, a young smiling man with long bleached hair, turns in his seat and shakes Alex's hand.

"Mrs. Parker, do you have any questions before we take off?" Mandy asks.

I'm out of my element here. "Not really," I tell her, "except that I wanted a chance to say goodbye to Alex."

"Oh, I'm sorry. I didn't mean to whisk him away before you could even say goodbye." She opens the door and I hesitantly step up into the bus. Alex stares at me, saying nothing, his eyes narrowed.

"Bye."

"Bye," Alex mumbles.

"Have fun," I say, immediately regretting I had said it. God, what a stupid remark that was. I loathe myself. Alex doesn't respond, and there is nothing left to say. I walk to the mile-marker post and stand there, raise a hand and hesitate, then wave as the buses drive away. I feel more isolated at this moment than ever in my entire life.

Feeling weak, I climb back into the van, fasten my seatbelt, and lay my head on the steering wheel. Where did I go wrong? The agony is sharp, more than I can bear, more than I bargained for. As I look down through the steering wheel, I notice my jeans straining at the seams, wipe my running mascara off onto a wad of Kleenex, and realize that Alex is not the only one that needs rescuing.

I make another, slower U-turn, the last one today, and drive toward home. At the Dairy Queen in Gooding, I sit inside a tissue-littered stall and cry like a mother who has lost her child forever. Bring him back to me, I plead silently, urgently, angrily demanding the God I have believed in all my life to listen to me for once.

Heading home, I am surprised at the numbness overtaking my grief. I don't feel sad. I don't feel much of anything, really, except for a vague sense of relief, of hope, perhaps.

The days pass and I go about my daily routine, but not without glancing in the direction of Alex's camp. I can see the mountains from my kitchen window and the valley beneath where Alex is toughing it out, and the questions prick at my conscience. Is it raining on him, too? Is he getting enough food? Is he getting his fires started? What does creek water taste like? Are there rattlesnakes in his camp? Does he think about us? Does he miss us? Does he hate us?

Alex's skin is brown, his fingernails long and encrusted with dirt. His hair springs out in wild ringlets about his deeply tanned face. Dirt is embedded in frown lines on his forehead. There is an earthy, pungent smell about him. His eyes are darker and more intense than usual.

We have come to attend the final ceremony where our son will be released back to us. He and the other boys demonstrate how to make fire, construct a backpack and lean-tos. Alex shows us his trophy—a set of rattlers from a snake he killed for his supper one night.

He stiffens when I hug him at the end of the ritual. "I smell," he says.

"It's not so bad," I say.

"I only got to bathe a couple of times, Mom."

"You're kidding."

"No, and I had to earn the privilege, too."

The group is excused to go shower before we can have them back. Afterward, we all drive out to a country restaurant just above the bank of the Snake River for an all-you-can-eat breakfast buffet. Alex orders a chocolate milkshake and a Coke and piles his plate high with eggs, bacon, biscuits, pancakes, and donuts. I watch as he drizzles sausage gravy over all of it, including the donuts. After eating a small fraction of the smorgasbord on his plate, he stops.

"All this food and I can't eat it," he says. "I'm already full." We laugh, and Alex is radiant. It's the first I've seen his grin in quite some time.

Later in the parking lot, the boys exchange e-mail addresses and cell phone numbers, and I fumble with the stone in the pocket of my worn out windbreaker. I touch it and hold it tightly as I have done off and on for the past three weeks. I don't want to let it go, but reluctantly I retrieve it back into the light.

"Remember this?" I once again offer it to Alex.

"Not really," he says, but there's a hint of recognition in his eyes and he smiles. He takes the stone and flips it over in his palm a few times. "Do you want it?"

"I think I can let go of it now," I say. "Let's see how far you can skip it across the Snake."

"Okay," Alex says, eyeing me in a quizzical manner, but his face transforms into a wide grin as he deftly flicks the stone in a straight line just above the surface of the water. With each skip across the river, the smooth white stone glistens in the morning sun until it hits the other side.

A BOY, A BAG,
A PAPER ROUTE

Judy Lockhart DiGregorio

S everal years ago, I discovered a paper route could be detrimental to a mother's health.

When our thirteen-year-old son, Chuck, announced his intention of becoming a paperboy for our daily paper, the *Oak Ridger,* we gave him our blessing. The *Oak Ridger* assigned him a route in the Emory Heights section of town, and Chuck proudly picked up his delivery bag made of green cotton fabric.

Each weekday afternoon after school, he pedaled off on his blue bicycle. He picked up his eighty papers about one-fourth mile from our house. Then he spent the next couple of hours delivering them.

It took time to learn the route and the idiosyncrasies of its customers. Some wanted their paper left on the front porch, some in the carport. Others wanted it placed beside the driveway or three inches to the left of the back step.

Collecting the monthly bill was another challenging experience. The customers who made the most money seemed to have the most excuses for not paying Chuck.

"Come back later. I only have a $100 bill."

"I'm sure I already paid you this month."

"Are you really my paperboy?"

Chuck was a dependable paperboy most of the time,

even though he occasionally threw papers on the roof or into the bushes. We always knew when he had a careless day because his customers phoned us to complain. We complained, too, to Chuck.

Chuck came down with mononucleosis toward the end of his sophomore year in high school. The doctor told him to stay home for one week and rest. Chuck found a substitute paperboy for the first four days of his route. However, he couldn't find anyone to deliver the papers on Friday afternoon.

His father, Dan, was coaching track, and his sister, Candie, had dance classes. I, his faithful mother, agreed to do the route after I returned home from work. Dan promised to come and help me after track practice.

Chuck told me where to find the papers. He gave me his customer list and handed me his green *Oak Ridger* bag. I pulled the strap over my head and marched outside, ready for delivery duty.

The temperature was seventy degrees. It was a great opportunity to be outdoors and help my son at the same time. With a smile on my face, I strolled leisurely up the block to the corner of Dayton and Carnegie.

I found several bundles of papers at the foot of a towering oak tree, just as Chuck said. Humming to myself, I removed the *Oak Ridger* bag and untied the twine on the bundles. Then I began to stuff all eighty papers into the bag. The Friday edition included the weekend section so the papers were thicker than usual.

The bag bulged dangerously at the seams, but I forced every single paper inside. Then I tried to hoist the bag up to place the strap over my head. It was heavier than expected, so I fell to my knees and tried again, resting the bag on the ground this time. The papers felt like cinder blocks.

Grabbing the tree trunk, I pulled myself up inch by inch. Finally, I stood hunched over like a Neanderthal woman. The bag weighed so much I couldn't keep my balance. How did a skinny guy like my son have the strength to lug this huge bag of papers around and pedal a bicycle at the same time?

Plunging bravely ahead, I pulled out my delivery list and wobbled down the road like a seasick giraffe. When I positioned the bag in front of me, I tilted forward. When I pushed the bag behind me, I leaned backward. The only way I could successfully control the bag was to perch it on my left hip and cling to it desperately as I lurched from side to side.

As I approached the first steep driveway on the route, I felt like Sisyphus pushing the rock up the mountain. This was not fun. It was hard work.

For every two or three papers I delivered, I collapsed on the curb to rest. Then I had to struggle upright again. I staggered up hills and fell down driveways. I skinned both knees trying to run away from a snarling white terrier. The load of papers grew heavier instead of lighter as my legs tired.

After two hours of torture, I was not even halfway done with the route. I wondered which level of Dante's *Inferno* I had entered and how long it was going to last.

Suddenly a voice yelled out behind me.

"Honey, are you drunk?" asked my husband, laughing. "You're teetering all over the road."

Then he noticed the *Oak Ridger* bag swollen with papers protruding from my hip.

"Did you put all eighty papers in the bag at one time?"

"Isn't that what I was supposed to do?" I snapped.

"Chuck delivers one-third of the papers at a time. Then he returns and gets another bunch. That bag must weigh a ton. No wonder you're staggering around."

"Well, I've never delivered Chuck's papers before. He didn't explain the process to me."

"Give me the bag, and I'll help you finish the route. With both of us doing it, maybe we'll be done before dark," Dan said.

Gratefully, I relinquished the bag, and we delivered the remaining *Oak Ridgers*. Trudging home, I moaned all the way. My back ached. My neck hurt. My feet throbbed.

As I fell asleep that Friday night, I prayed fervently for Chuck's swift recovery so he could resume his paper route.

A mother will do anything for her child, but this mother will only do it once.

FIVE EMPTY CHAIRS
Nancy Fletcher-Blume

M y kitchen table is
pushed against the wall,
guarded by five empty chairs.

The visitors that come will leave no
fingerprints in the dust.
It's crowded memories surrounding my table
not allowing me to sit.

In solitude, I watch
shadowy figures in the chairs
moving away from me, until there's
room for me
to see
just a kitchen table, pushed
against the wall
guarded by five empty chairs.

In memory of Ray, David, and Bobby

THE ONE AND ONLY ESCAPADE
OF THE PINE-PANEL KID
Mary Frazier Brennan

Most kids wait until they're sixteen or seventeen before sneaking out of the house and getting pulled over by the cops. I did it at four.

The summer of 1955 was hot, humid, and gnat-peppered in the little town of Perry, Georgia. We'd made the move from the thriving metropolis of Chattanooga, Tennessee, to slower-paced Perry in the fall of 1954, when Daddy got a job at nearby Warner Robbins Air Force Base. A mint-green and white ranch house awaited us on Pine Ridge Drive in a newly planted subdivision about a mile from the center of town. In a valiant attempt to outwit the heat and the gnats, my daddy converted the screened-in porch on the side of the house into a den, complete with pine paneling. Of all the fascinating pine-sort-of-things connected with our new home, pine paneling was the most intriguing to me. I don't know what that says about me as a four-year-old, but there you have it.

I wasn't supposed to overhear the conversation between my mother and my brother that summer afternoon. What I was supposed to be doing was taking a nap. An A-type personality from birth, I wasn't really into napping as a kid, though I've more than made up for it in my dotage. Still, Mother thought I was drowsily settled in with my two-year-old sister in our bedroom, and bless her heart, I let her believe that. But my eavesdropping paid off when I heard my brother whine and balk after Mother asked him to run into town and pick up some pins for her. Ears a-perk, I started hatching my plan. The prospects of escaping the confines of a nap-room and doing a good deed at the same time were just too alluring. Call it fate. Call it kismet. Call it misbehaving. I was up for it.

Sneaking out wasn't really that hard. Dressed only in baggy white underpants—remember, it's summer in middle Georgia—I scuttled right out the front door. Nobody even noticed. Once out of the house, I hopped onto my trusty trike and headed down the street toward downtown. I couldn't for the life of me understand why my brother would pass up an opportunity like this, freewheelin' down the street—no worries, no cares. The world at my little bare feet.

I pedaled for all I was worth toward town and must have stayed on the sidewalks, stopped at the stop signs, and looked both ways before scooting across the streets, because I arrived safe and sound. Nobody stopped me along the way to say, "Hey, little girl, where are you going, dressed only in your underpants? Does your mama know where you are?" Nope. Nary a one. I suppose a scantily clad kid enjoying a ride on her tricycle on a summer's afternoon just didn't raise any red flags in 1955. So I cruised into Perry's main shopping district carefree, independent, and secure in the knowledge that I was on a sacred mission. I knew the way to the dime store, and despite the lunch-hour traffic rush, was having the time of my short life.

Everything was ticking along just fine until that police car slowed to a stop right next to me. A lanky policeman— taking his own sweet time, I suppose, so as not to scare me right out of what little apparel I was wearing—got out of the car.

"So." (It was more like, "Soooooooooo.") "What's your name?" he asked.

I told him.

"Do you know where you live?" he continued.

"Yes, I sure do," I said, puffing out my four-year-old naked chest. "I live on Pine Panel Drive." Pine Ridge, Pine Panel—all the same to a kid. And anyway, I knew more about pine paneling than I did pine ridges at the time. Still do.

I don't remember the policeman's reaction to that nugget of information. Was he amused? Did he repeat the question to see if he'd heard me right the first time? I do not know. But I will never forget what happened next. Just as the police grilling reached its climax, I saw my brother cross the street on his bicycle, presumably on his way to get the pins for Mother. Now, when I say he was crossing the street, he wasn't crossing toward me, to rescue his baby sister. No siree. He saw Little Sister had been pulled over by the cops, so he was high-tailin' it in the opposite direction. Neither of us acknowledged the other, but I will never forget the look of surprised terror on his face as he surveyed the situation. I could practically hear the screaming inside my brother's head: *Do I rescue her or do I run for my life? Rescue or run? Rescue or run?* He opted for RUN.

But let me tell you, it didn't concern me one little bit that he'd panicked and fled the scene. I was handling things very nicely and could cope with this police guy on my own. The only thing that bothered me was that my brother would get the errand done while I was standing around jawing with one of Perry's finest. It just wasn't my day to do a good deed.

After several more questions, the policeman finished up his interrogation, convinced he had sufficient information regarding my ability to lead him to my house on Pine Panel Drive. He chucked me and my tricycle into the police car and off we went. I was duly delivered to the mint-green and white ranch house with a pine-paneled den on Pine Ridge Drive, none the worse for wear and secure in the knowledge that should the situation come up again, I could get to town to get the job done.

Naturally, it became the stuff of family legends and grown-up analysis, eliciting guffaws and knowing winks, always pointing up that razor-thin line between adorably funny and deadly dangerous. And of course it foretold all sorts of things about me—the independence, the wanderlust, the innate sense of direction, a pine panel den of my own. All except the topless thing. I never had the courage to do that much beyond my Perry days. Truly.

The only part of the tale that's kind of embarrassing for this card-carrying Baby Boomer is that my only rebellious, cheeky run-in with the fuzz was at the ripe old age of four. On the other hand, it just might be fair warning for whoever will be looking after me in my declining years. So, to whatever brave soul is stuck with me in the future, a little advice: keep the doors locked and hide the tricycle.

Oh, and be prepared—I may be topless.

SCARLETT
L. Ward Abel

This locality
has no feeling for the past,
its victories or mistakes.
I sense that forgetting
has become the philosophy of the "New" South.
There are subdivisions
that have been placed upon battlefields,
and one was built on the old Fitzgerald plantation
where Margaret Mitchell used to spend
her summers,
conjuring Tara and the O'Hara's. But not even a
plaque remains there on the corner of Folsom Road.
While attempting to snuff out evil,
we have opted for a more insidious plantation
devoid of roots
and memory.

FARM NEIGHBORS
S. R. Lee

When the raw wood framing of houses began rising like strange blond trespassers two fields over beyond the barn, Martha shuddered from their unspoken threats, but found no words to explain her fear.

"Look," she said to William at breakfast. "They've bulldozed down those trees. Mrs. Everett had a shady pasture back there." Mrs. Everett had been her grandmother's best friend, the grandmother who left Martha the farm. Martha grieved that Mrs. Everett had to sell her place to pay for upkeep in a nursing home.

But William muttered, "Machines need space to work."

When each new house began to show its pale yellow wood and odd blue insulation panels rising beyond the pig lot, Martha would try again.

"Look, William, at how—" but she could never quite finish her sentence. *Strange* was too weak a word for what she was feeling.

"Don't be so worried," William told her. "Land values rise when people move out here, but as long as I keep farming, we'll be taxed as agricultural. Our kids'll go to college on this land's worth."

"I'm keeping their college money. They can both go to State without selling our land."

A few days later, William said, "From up on the silo, that subdivision looks just like a little toy town. You ought to see it."

But Martha was not thinking of climbing any silo. She shivered when she overheard Jamie and Fran outside the kitchen window.

"Jamie, please, please," Fran was whining. "I'll make you brownies with mint icing. He thinks you're old enough to go up. I'll hold on tight and not look down. I'll never tell."

"Dad would kill me if I took you up that silo," Jamie growled. But as the two children walked away, Martha felt that Fran's pleas might prevail.

Martha watched closely at supper. When the subject of those houses came up, Fran stuffed a biscuit in her mouth. That should keep her gagged until the dangerous subject had passed. Jamie, at fifteen, was a real help with farm work, so he could skip some rules, but if they should ever let slip that nine-year-old Fran had climbed that silo, William would switch her good. He was a practical farmer who didn't hold with children not keeping rules.

The silo view of the growing toy town seemed to make William and the children more at ease about all that commotion beyond the fields. Only Martha from her limited view at the kitchen window felt disaster in the new world beginning there. Even beyond the barn, the pig lot, and the wide alfalfa field, the new construction intruded on her world. She could not imagine why families wanted to live in such big houses.

So when on a Sunday afternoon William said, "Let's go take a look at the new places, get our gawking done before they move in," Martha hoped a closer look would make her feel better. They all four walked together up the new road where huge machines roared and beeped during the week.

Fran had brought the dogs and was racing with them up and back on the unfamiliar scraped ground. Martha warned her, "Don't run in people's yards."

But William said, "Don't matter yet. They haven't put down turf, haven't even paved the driveways. Maybe you'll have some friends up here, Frannie. Look around and get used to it."

Martha focused on the half-finished houses.

"If those women keep their jobs in town, how will I meet them?"

But no one heard her. William was studying a half-basement design new to him, Fran had run on with the dogs, and Jamie was admiring some dormer windows. Martha felt no sense of people here yet, but maybe they would seem real to her when their children came to the school or if some of the families came to church.

"There's no life in this place. I guess it'll be better once they move in."

"Oh, they'll get here soon enough, and then you'll be bringing over bread and garden sweet corn or ripe tomato relish like you always do with new folks."

Martha supposed so. William seemed easy enough with this new world.

Strangers were walking on the new road, too. Martha could hear their comments.

"Too steep, don't want to be slipping in the snow."

"Good, big trees—can we get the house on it without cutting them?"

"Well, those two will have to go, but that big one might be back far enough."

Martha wondered how the trees felt, hearing their deaths discussed.

"I don't know about this school," another woman was saying. "Maybe I'll just drive the kids to town."

We have a nice school, Martha thought. Are they moving here without even finding out?

Watching two boys kick a soccer ball, Martha thought ahead to the fall. Some of those kids would be on the school bus with Fran. She hoped they weren't rough.

The soccer ball almost collided with the dogs. When William whistled them to heel, Fran came to walk beside her mother.

"That boy didn't look. It wasn't Rex's fault," she said.

"The boys didn't mean any harm," Martha tried to be reassuring. "Smile. They'll be on the school bus with you next fall, and they'll be wanting a friendly face."

"I always sit with Alice."

Alice had been Fran's best friend since kindergarten.

"You and Alice need to be friendly to these new people. Make them feel welcome and things will go better."

Jamie had always protected Fran from any rough teasing on the bus, but this fall he planned to ride to high school in a friend's truck. Martha hoped there wouldn't be teenagers driving from the new houses. She always worried when a car went fast toward that curve by the creek.

"William, won't this mean more traffic on our road?"

"A good bit, Martha. I'll cut back more brush from the driveway turn."

In May, families moved into three new houses near the main road. Mud was still deep in the yards, and their clean cars sat uneasily on the paved driveways. The mothers seemed to be driving their children into town every morning.

Martha supposed they didn't want to change schools right at the end of the year. She'd do the same for Fran. Still, going away every day kept them strangers to the neighborhood.

Well into June, Martha still couldn't quite bring herself to go over with some early corn from her garden and knock on the new doors, although she thought that was what a good neighbor should do.

"Tomorrow," she would say to Fran, "we need to take some of these green beans and a jar of last year's pickles over to that new house on the corner."

But somehow on the next day, Martha was busy with freezing the early corn, and Fran was off on her bike to Alice's.

Those new people didn't seem to bother William a bit until the day he saw five children down in the creek by old Ed Forrest's place.

"What in the world?"

Ed Forrest was always cross with children.

"They'd better watch out—Old Ed's quick with a shotgun."

"They've been down there all week, Daddy," Fran volunteered. "They say they're building a dam to make a swimming hole."

"You didn't go down there, Fran? You know not to go on Mr. Forrest's place." Now William did sound worried.

"Mama was taking me to 4-H. We heard them shouting in the creek."

William looked at Martha. "Why didn't you tell me?"

"You just don't seem to understand, William. I've had this bad feeling ever since those houses started, but I can't explain it to you."

"Well, let's hope Ed's temper doesn't get the best of him. Maybe we should speak to those parents."

"Oh, William, we don't even know their names." Martha knew he was right, but she didn't want to go alone. "Both of us need to go."

"Not this week—weather's dry enough to make hay."

By the time William and Jamie had the huge round hay bales lined up along the edge of the field, Martha was busy freezing the green beans that were doing so well in the garden, and Fran was making practice batches of brownies for the 4-H contest at the Fourth of July picnic. As the family dealt with the constant work of summer, they forgot to worry about subdivision children.

On the Fourth of July, however, the new people were bothersome. Before daylight, Martha was wakened by some faraway shooting that kept on and on. Only when William muttered, "Damn kids!" did she realize the shooting sound was coming from the subdivision.

"Fireworks?" she asked.

"Glad our kids are raised right."

William allowed fireworks only in the evening under his careful oversight.

"Summer's half gone and we don't know them yet. Funny to have neighbors stay strangers so long." Martha felt guilty that she had done nothing to welcome them, but this was to be a busy day.

Without being in the county school, none of the new children would be at the 4-H picnic. She guessed they didn't have much else to do, other than shoot firecrackers.

"Frannie'll take all morning to get those brownies ready."

"Well, I have plenty to take Jamie's time."

The popping noises from the subdivision went on all morning while Martha was stuffing eggs for the picnic, while Fran was packing her brownies, while Martha was frying chicken, while Jamie was washing the car, while Martha was mixing up the bean salad. She wasn't surprised that William came in with a headache frown between his eyes.

The ordinary daily happiness of Martha's summer ended that afternoon. When the women were sitting in the shade, all the dinner eaten and the men and children busy with a ball game, Sherrie Everly launched into a tale about her cousins. "They came *that* close to losing their farm over by Smith's Corner. Some Boy Scout troop camping in the state park came over into Cousin Burke's woods. This one boy got himself up in a tree. Then he fell out and broke his arm."

"So? It wasn't Burke's fault."

"The insurance company sued. They have big time lawyers. The jury gave the boy's parents the medical bills and then some more for pain and suffering. Burke's lawyer said it wasn't Burke's fault if he didn't even know the scouts were there, but the judge said he was lucky the boy hadn't broken his back, or they would have had to pay a whole lot more. So they paid, then put out No Trespassing signs all around their farm."

"Maybe we'd better get some, too?"

Worried remarks floated among the women.

"Martha, you're over by that new subdivision. You ever see those people?"

"Well, not much." But then she remembered those children on the road and in the creek.

She mentioned the lawsuit to William that night when they were alone. "Sherrie's cousin over by Smith's Corner was sued."

"I heard about that. Better get some signs next time we're in town."

"Will it make any difference?"

"Judge Bailey said it would. He told everybody to get some. Said subdivision people sue when they get hurt."

"I'll get some tomorrow."

She could tell he wasn't really worried like he ought to be.

On her way to the hardware store the next day, she saw the children walking strung out down the road. One she guessed to be twelve years old was walking with two others a little younger. Far behind them came two small ones with bright blond hair, maybe four-year-olds, wearing sunsuits and walking slowly because they were barefoot. The lead boy carried a fishing pole and had two fancy flies stuck in the band of his hat. What did he expect to catch in that little shallow creek? He ignored the little ones walking out in the road, so Martha slowed her car beside them. She rolled down her window and said, "Be careful. Stay over on the side." She didn't want to seem scolding, but the children were really out in the road.

"We need those signs put up," she told William later.

"Promise I'll get 'em up before hunting season for sure. Don't want those men thinking our woods are for just anybody to hunt in."

Now Martha thought again she should get to know her new neighbors, maybe tell them how dangerous William's sows would be when the piglets came and that the poke-berries along their back fences were poison. But surely they knew that. She shouldn't be thinking people were stupid just because she didn't know them. She felt shy, somehow, when she went past that new road. The shiny cars that passed the house so fast made Martha feel the people were different. She wouldn't know what to say. But she really should find the mothers of the little ones and tell them how the children walked in the road.

In mid-August, school started and some new children caught the bus at the end of their road.

Fran said, "They know a lot."

"How can you tell, you've just been in school one day," Jamie teased.

"Mr. Smarty! One new boy's been to Disneyland, even swum in the ocean. Anybody you know done that?"

As the weeks went on, Martha sometimes asked, "What's the new boy like?"

"He's good at reading and at math, too," Fran was visibly impressed that day.

But a few days later she said, "He doesn't know how to talk about much except his own trips."

"Give him time," Martha told her. "When he's been in school a while, he'll get interested in something here."

But Martha wondered. She hadn't seen new families much at the grocery or the farm supply store. None of them had shown up at Willow Grove Baptist Church in spite of the new welcome sign. If the new people didn't come around, how were they to know folks? The only ones she saw were the two blond little ones who didn't yet go to school. They had been on the edge of the road twice by themselves. She always slowed her car and waved.

The hot end of summer was upon them. The pigs had farrowed successfully. The pig lot was covered with squealing little piglets, running here and there, their mothers anxiously looking about. They were noisy in the mornings, pushing near the feed troughs. Martha wondered if the neighbors could hear them. Would pig squeals bother those people like the fireworks had bothered William?

"Have to get rid of half of them soon," William said. "Lot'll be so crowded they can't get to their feed. Stay away from them, Fran."

"Oh, Daddy! I do. It's too muddy out there anyway."

William didn't get around to putting up the ten No Trespassing signs stacked on the back porch.

"That'll be a job for Jamie some Saturday before deer season."

"Can you hunt with those houses so close?" Martha suddenly had a new worry.

"We've always hunted. I got folks counting on me for deer. Can't stop us from living on our own land." William's anger made Martha know he was worried, too.

With school in session, Martha felt easier. The new children were in class all day, so she didn't see them in the creek. On Saturdays, William made sure his children did their chores and studied for good grades, so Jamie and Fran were at home most of the time, though Fran and Alice managed to get together just as if they hadn't seen each other all week. Most of the garden was in the freezer; it was time to think about the Fall Festival at school.

"Mama, I said at school you'd take a booth."

"Oh, Frannie, did you really have to say that?"

"Mama, please do the cakewalk. It's more fun than those booths where you throw things."

Martha telephoned quickly to the festival chairman and sure enough got the cakewalk.

The next day, Fran campaigned and came home triumphant.

"Alice and Sarah and Maggie and June Rae all said their mamas will make cakes, and then I asked the boys, and Stanley and Dickie said they'd ask because they like cake.

But Mama, that new boy just said 'What's a cake walk?' Doesn't he know?"

"Well, Frannie, those subdivision people have a lot to learn. We'll show him a real good one this year."

The cakewalk always had a cheerful crowd. People were good about giving cakes to it, and grownups as well as children wanted to get in the circle and walk until the music stopped.

On the Thursday afternoon before the Festival, Martha's cakes were sitting in boxes, all ready for Friday night. After two hard days of rain, this morning the air had been dry, so her icing had set quite well.

Martha found paper, pen, and scissors to make tickets. While she sat at the kitchen table, she glanced out from time to time to the new roofs beyond the barn and the pig lot. The yellow sunlight of autumn always made her think of some poem she'd read in school, though she couldn't remember its name.

But now a quick storm was brewing. The wind had picked up and a heavy cloud was rolling in from the west.

Two bright little flashes caught her eye. At first they were like some queer dream, two moving bits of yellow among the dark pigs. Then a child turned, and Martha saw they were real—the two smallest children from the new houses were in the muddy lot among the mother sows and piglets. Martha ran, but stopped at the back steps. If she frightened the sows, the children would have no chance. She should go through the barn and call to the children carefully from the hallway. With her view blocked by the barn, she only heard the young voice shout, "Catch that one!"

As she ran again, heavy rain began to pound. She dashed to the fence without feeling it.

She was too late. Mud must have choked the children's cries when the big sows attacked. With the bloody scene tearing through her mind, Martha turned back, huddling against the rough boards of the barn. By the time she looked up again, the pig lot was a confusion of mud with several sows rooting together in one spot, nothing left to see at all.

Martha didn't know what to do. There was nothing to save after the sows had chewed and trampled. Whom should she tell? What should she tell them? A lawsuit would take everything they had.

The children had completely disappeared. Police dogs couldn't follow a scent after such a hard rainstorm. William and Jamie joined the neighborhood men in searching the woods and checking up and down the creek. Martha took her turn manning the telephone hot line. The subdivision parents seemed to appreciate how much their farm neighbors were ready to help in a crisis.

All through the winter, Martha carefully watched the mud of the pig lot for buttons or bits of bone.

NOSTALGIA RESIDES IN THE MARROW

William W. Fraker

Nostalgia resides in the marrow and sinews of cows
 Who know the path and time of milking
   long before the bark
Of the collie. Most congregate behind the barn,
Waiting the parting of the wide sliding aluminum doors.
Followers, branded with marked ears and the
   jingling pendants
Of the devout, proceed in full expectation of relief
From their bloating and their hunger. Like infants,
Hummed to sleep by miles of highway,
Bovinity seeks a deeper peace that awakens in sensuousness,
Of crushed gravel and ruts recognized
As the beginning of home's familiar drive.

Earlier in the afternoon, Grandfather hoisted watermelons
Out from a creek, where they had been stashed to cool.
Sweetness and moist sunlight were sliced and distributed.
Seeds were spread on the back concrete steps,
Close to shadows where the hound dogs sought refuge.
Reaching into the side of his khakis, Grandfather glances
At his pocket watch and dons the boots of a celebrant
Continuing his service at the barn, with a Vespers
Pungent with life's abundance.

SIMPLE PLEASURES
Ginger Manley

The cardboard box—particularly one large enough to create a "home" for a child whose imagination can be unleashed with some scissors and markers—has recently been honored by induction into the National Toy Hall of Fame. A summer visit from Alexander, our six-year-old grandson, suggests that there may be some other nominees.

While earlier generations of grandchildren received rattles and teddy bears, Alexander's first toy had been a cell phone and later, with better eye-hand coordination, he played with joysticks. Before he could talk in sentences, he could reprogram his parents' video system and play interactive computer games.

So it was with some trepidation that his grandfather and I anticipated entertaining Alexander for a week in our electronically challenged home. It's not that we still play 78's on turntables and listen to 8-track cassettes—although we do still have these around—but we are not the most "techie" of grandparents.

It was only a few months earlier that I had seen a friend walking with a small white rectangular device hanging on a lanyard around her neck. I inquired if she had a new piece of medical equipment and was chastened to be told, "No, it's an I-pod." It took a few more weeks before I got the courage to ask someone, "What is an I-pod?"

Grandpa and I thought it best to forewarn Alexander's parents so they could pack all the necessary equipment to prevent their son from a serious case of "electronic gadget withdrawal." Obligingly, he arrived for his visit with his own portable DVD player and discs, his Game-Boy, and his personal night-light in tow. Unfortunately, the battery recharger and back-up battery pack for the DVD player did not arrive with him. The Game-Boy broke in a couple of days. Luckily, the night-light only required a wall source of 110-volt electric current and we could supply that amenity.

Despite these potential pitfalls, the week sped by— staying up late after catching lightning bugs, sleeping in in the mornings, listening to the snap-crackle-pop of our Rice Krispies, and eating grilled cheese sandwiches with chocolate milk for lunch and maybe also for supper. Dusty boxes of Chutes and Ladders and Candyland games from the attic competed with innumerable rounds of Uno and Old Maid.

With lots of brush piles to be disposed of from ongoing yard work, Alexander and Grandpa stayed busy loading the pickup truck and driving together the mile or so to the landfill where they could deposit the limbs and twigs in the designated dumpsters.

On one of these daily excursions to the dump, Grandpa's cell phone—not the latest attached-to-the-hip model, but a bulky 90's version that had to be carried in the chest pocket of his shirt—inadvertently was dumped into the bin with the yard debris when he bent to give it the last heave-ho. This created an eye-popping experience for Alexander to watch his granddad get completely inside the bin to retrieve the phone, which he located by ringing it twenty-six times from my cell phone.

When the boys arrived back home, Grandpa was literally black from head to foot, covered with some of the soot he had dumped. I met him at the door to the kitchen and ordered him to take off his filthy clothes in the garage before he entered the house. Seeing that his underwear was no cleaner than the outerwear, I furthermore instructed him to strip completely and go outside so I could wash him off with the hose.

"You're going to make Grandpa get naked and hose him off, Grandma?" the startled Alexander asked me.

We found another solution to this situation before the neighbors were exposed to a new form of geriatric recreation, but the whole event created an opportunity for Alexander's fertile mind. At bedtime he asked if, instead of getting in the bathtub that night, he could just get naked and have me hose him off.

Grandpa and I thought the county fair would be a great opportunity to continue to imbue this little California boy with our rural Tennessee culture. Our initial visit to the mule barn seemed to be less impressive for him than we had hoped, but he did like the Ferris Wheel and the Pirates' Ship ride. For all three of us, seeing the Human Cannonball soar out of his rocket launcher and land in a net over our heads was a pretty cool first-ever-in-our-lifetime experience. Cotton candy and corn dogs completed the cultural immersion—not exactly Legoland or Sea World, but pretty good in our book.

We rounded out the week with running through the sprinklers, cutting zinnias for the dinner table, eating corn on the cob—or in Alexander's case, corn off the cob since it is pretty much impossible to make a dent in an ear of Silver Queen if you are missing four of your front teeth. And with all this, not a single symptom of gadget withdrawal.

On the last night of vacation, our family custom is to ask each other "What did you like best about our time together?" Grandpa said he liked the Human Cannonball best, and I said I liked lying in the hammock with Alexander and the lightning bugs just before he released them to their homes.

"What was your favorite thing we did in Tennessee, Alexander?"

Thinking hard, he eventually answered, "Well, my third favorite thing we did was when me and Grandpa washed out the pickup truck and then rolled it out in the driveway and you put the mattress from the camping stuff in the garage in it and we all laid down and watched the stars come out."

"Awwhh!"

We'd done well, and Grandpa and I winked at each other and he reached for my hand.

"So what was your second favorite thing?"

"My second favorite thing was watching Grandpa dive the dumpster."

"Oops."

We didn't mean for that one to stay with him.

"And your most favorite thing that you did on your Tennessee vacation?"

Long silence, then a smile that can only be described as a "miraculous epiphany."

"My most favorite thing of all was when I was running through the sprinklers and I had to go potty and you didn't want me to track the wet grass into the house, so I got to pee in the yard!"

Why was I not surprised to hear that upon starting first grade at Our Immaculate Lady Grammar School the week after he returned home, Alexander's story on "what I did on my summer vacation" began with "I visited my grandparents in Tennessee, where my grandpa dives dumpsters, and I peed in the yard and got hosed off every night before we all laid down to sleep together on the old mattress that Grandma drug out of the garage and put in the bed of the pickup truck."

If only I had saved for him the cardboard box that my new refrigerator was delivered in a few days before his arrival, then he could have also told the nuns in detail about the corrugated architecture of his room at his grandparents.

SMALL TOWN REVERIE
Jennifer Dix

He had one arm propped on the steering wheel of the blue Chevy pickup. I saw him give me the signal as our vehicles met on Highway 89, heading in opposite directions. It was a quick flick of the wrist and an upward extension of hand and fingers. For a split second the casual acknowledgment surprised me, but then I remembered that I had used the same gesture when I had once called this town home. At that moment it occurred to me that this offhand wave was like some sort of rural code. It was just something people living in small towns did when meeting other cars on the road. I reciprocated the wave for the rest of my weekend visit, and each time, I smiled at the simplicity and civility of it all.

Traffic lights are nonexistent here. Two state highways intersect in the middle of town, and a commanding STOP sign holds solitary reign over the junction. An old school friend's parents own Larry's Service Station in one corner of the intersection. A rickety backless bench with vanishing remnants of blue paint sits behind the two gas pumps, and the older gentlemen in their worn Big Ben overalls would convene there every weekday afternoon. They'd watch the cars and buses pass from school letting out and reminisce about the old days or discuss the year's crop yields, while spitting Red Man tobacco into soiled tin cans. Mr. Larry would pump gas or patch flat tires while customers waited, then smile and say "alrighty, we'll do" when asked to "please put it on my bill."

I don't remember much about the tiny grocery store, except that it was sufficiently named The Store and had uneven wooden floors and an old Formica bar with worn red leather and chrome barstools. I had to hang on for dear life to stay aboard those wobbly stools while Mom purchased a pound of rag bologna, a 2-liter RC Cola, and a box of Little Debbie's to take home for lunch. Tacked to the walls behind the cash register were high school basketball schedules, newspaper clippings, and school pictures. Kitchen staples and basic grocery needs could be filled there until it went out of business several years ago. I still wonder what happened to those red barstools.

The Volunteer Fire Department was one of the newer buildings in town during my younger days, and it doubled as a community center. Numerous bridal teas, baby showers, and town meetings were held in the room adjacent to the fire engines. My eighteen-year-old self would never have guessed that the same parking lot where I washed cars with my senior classmates would be the same black asphalt everyone would park on when I had my own bridal shower there five years later.

There was one bank in town, and on Friday paydays the line at the single drive-up window wound around the corner and out into the shoulder of the highway. Inside, little ones looked forward to peering over the counter at the teller, certain to score a Dum-Dum lollipop or a couple of pieces of wintergreen gum in a tiny cardboard box. I was one of many kids who graduated from leaving the bank with a lollipop to leaving with a loan payment receipt or a savings account book.

The post office was in a small tan brick building on the opposite side of the highway from the bank. I would go in and wait in line at the counter for Mr. Hugh, the Postmaster, and stare at the speckled mud-brown tile floor or the FBI Wanted posters on the corkboard. Mrs. McDaniel opened a florist shop in the same building and did a booming business on Valentine's Day, when many of the high school kids ordered helium balloons and flowers to be delivered to a boyfriend, girlfriend, or crush of the week. It was a proud day when the more modern post office was built, but most would admit that the new building lacked the character of the original and certainly didn't include the convenience of a florist shop next door.

Another friend's family owned Perry's Farm Supply, situated across from Larry's Service Station. The Mill kept the local farming community in feed, grain augers, and veterinary supplies, and a few high school boys in jobs and spending money. It smelled of grain, corn dust, and simple unadulterated country life. Dad would drive his Ford pickup, Ol' Red, into the covered bay, and my brother and I would turn around in the seat and watch as Dad helped load the truck bed with enough feed to keep our rabbits, chickens, and various critters happy for another few weeks.

CJ's Restaurant had the casual dining market cornered. It sat in a large gravel lot across the street from The Store and was the favorite hangout for bored teenagers. We ate burgers and fries inside or sat on the hoods of cars out front, partaking in adolescent gossip and trying to decide what to do and where to go next. It was the place for the girls to be seen wearing their boyfriend's letter jacket, the boys to show off their new car stereo system, and either gender to prove their pool skills or arcade game expertise.

There are two churches in the immediate vicinity of town, the Church of Christ and the Baptist. While Dad led the singing at the Church of Christ, I sat in the front pew in my hopelessly dingy lace ankle socks and scuffed Mary Janes, sneaking glances at the clock to see how much longer until I could go outside and challenge the boys to a foot race in the parking lot. Congregations in the area let out at noon on Sundays, making this the most likely time for any sort of so-called traffic congestion, second only to weekdays at three o'clock when school dismissed.

The school was the heartbeat of the community and the life force that held it all together. The red brick building contained kindergarten through twelfth grades under one roof. I was in the first kindergarten class when it was built in the 1980s, and my brother was in the last graduating class of nine students before the school board voted to consolidate in 1997. The building is still standing, but each time I drive by on the way to my parents' house, it seems to be just a little more derelict, a little more neglected than the time before.

The cavernous gymnasium was hallowed ground and holds a celebrated place in my memory. The gym was where I spent most of my time, when not in class. I played on the basketball team every year from fifth through twelfth grades and was fiercely loyal to the sport, although not exactly MVP material. The wooden floor was buffed and polished to honey-golden perfection. The guidance counselor/English teacher was recruited to paint center court with our mascot, a black and gold eyepatch-wearing pirate clenching a dagger between his teeth. The bleachers were massive wooden benches set in concrete, painted black and then gray in later years. They lined the full length of both sides of the gym and rose up to meet the high windows near the ceiling. At one end of the basketball court was the stage where many school plays, beauty pageants, and graduation ceremonies were held.

The community fair took place on the school grounds every September and was the largest school fundraising event of the year. The kickoff was the Miss Fairest of the Fair beauty pageant held the night before. On Fair Day each grade's room showcased examples of students' classwork. The elementary students would display their handwriting samples, and the middle-schoolers were assigned history projects with blue and red ribbons given to the most creative. My fragile sixth grade ego was crushed when the three-foot totem pole I'd spent many weekends constructing by covering a cardboard tube with salt dough and bright primary colors didn't win a ribbon. Outdoors, the high school students raised money for their class coffers with various games, dunking booths, or face painting, while the PTO manned the concession stand and tempted passersby with grilled hamburgers, popcorn, candy, and fountain sodas. The 7:00 p.m. junior high basketball game against the same neighboring school every year marked the culmination of another school fair.

As my weekend visit came to an end, I drove through town for a last look and reflected on how much it had changed. Many of the businesses had closed down, and their windows were dark, hollow eye sockets peering out into the streets. The school no longer echoed with the squeak of sneakers on the basketball court, voices of first graders reciting their letters, or locker doors slamming. The energy seemed to have been drained from the streets and buildings. As I drove slowly by CJ's Restaurant, I met a man driving a John Deere tractor, going home after a long day in the field. He wiped his forehead with a red bandana, our eyes met, and I knew what to do. We flicked our wrists, and our fingers briefly pointed in a general upward direction, and that was it—the encounter was complete. I smiled again and was reassured that at the very least, the signal had endured.

78'S

Thomas D. Reynolds

A Victrola sits upstairs,
filled with 78's from the 1920's.
My grandpa traded a mule for them.

What glorious music must have meant
to a house etched in silence!

At Thanksgiving, the room crowded,
we play a few of our favorites—
Gid Tanner and the Skillet Lickers—
more for the name than the music,
their banjoes swallowed in static.

Later we sit around and tell stories.
My father begins to slide out his favorites,
so worn in the groove no one listens anymore,
needles skipping along the acetate,
scratching at the edges when the tune ends,
while the record keeps turning and turning.

As the room grows silent, I debate whether
I would trade a mule for these stories—

a good mule, hardworking, which rarely kicks—
and I decide to let the fields go to hell.

The nights are too long between four walls,
listening to wind in the trees,
staring at lines on your hands,
with a growing sense of isolation,
trying to think of the next word.

MISS JUANITA BRIDGES
Lonnye Sue Sims Pearson

M iss Juanita Bridges lived across the street and up a little alley from me when I was growing up in the Mississippi Delta. She lived in a four-room, wood-frame house perched on a tiny lot between Third and Fourth Avenues. I don't remember anything about her except she could make THE BEST fruit preserves I've ever put in my mouth.

Sometime around 1959, Miss Juanita began delivering pear, peach, and fig preserves to our door. Every jar contained nectar of the gods. Suspended in sweet, transparent syrup, the pears and peaches and figs languished in lusciousness— and they called my name. I swear they did!

For the first time in my life, someone other than my mother or my grandmother captured my culinary interest. Until Miss Juanita's preserves, I thought no one could cook or can as well as the women in my family. My grandmother's watermelon rind pickles and chow-chow were to die for, and Mama's hot pepper sauce simply could not be beaten, but Miss Juanita cornered the market with her fruit preserves . . . especially the pears.

Every spring when the fruit trees bloomed, I would walk across the street and stand staring at the buds that promised more preserves, watching those trees and willing the fruit to burst forth. Miss Juanita usually sat on her tiny front porch in a metal glider and watched the trees with me. We connected over fruit trees. I'd ask how long before the trees would have fruit instead of blooms. She'd answer with a laugh and say, "Oh, not too very long."

Trees surrounded her cottage, leaving just enough space for a tiny garden in which she grew all manner of vegetables. I knew about gardens. Mama and Daddy always had a garden with Kentucky Wonder pole beans and Big Boy tomatoes and crookneck squash and miles of weeds to hoe, so Miss Juanita's garden never really interested me. Gardens meant work to me. It was the fruit trees that captured my attention.

The days Miss Juanita canned, the aroma filled the neighborhood and my mouth watered. It won't be long now, I would think, and then I'd count the jars of preserves left in Mama's pantry. Many times I feared we would run out before the new batch came in, but we never did. Mama carefully guarded those pint-sized Mason jars filled with sunshine and summer rain and rich Delta soil and always managed to time it just right.

Mama made a big pan of biscuits the morning after the first delivery, and I relished opening the first jar of pear preserves of the year. My mouth still waters just thinking about smothering one of Mama's biscuits with the tantalizingly sweet syrup and precision-cut pears.

The day I left home in 1971, Miss Juanita walked across the street carrying a brown paper bag. Inside were four jars of pear preserves, one jar of peach preserves, and one jar of fig preserves. She handed the bag to me and said, "I know how much you like these so I decided to give you the first batch." For years after that, when she delivered her jewels to Mama, she added two extra jars of pear preserves "for Lonnye Sue." And I learned to guard those pint jars to make them last as long as possible.

Last summer I walked across the street and up the alley to stand in front of the tiny lot. The house is gone now— it finally fell into serious disrepair and had to be torn down. The fig tree is still there, but the peach trees are gone. There is one pear tree left. What I wouldn't give for one more jar of Miss Juanita's pear preserves and one of Mama's biscuits.

ROBERTA
L. Ward Abel

S he always visits
little bone yards
along state routes,
tracing paper in hand,
headstone occupants
bespoken with charcoal
and onionskin.
Names only names,
dates as bookends,
resolution implied from numbers, letters . . .
but how much of the story
can be retold from a rote?
How much of the lost brain
is fired,
saved
by her ritual?
Does she channel
with pencil
the senses
that have since
rejoined all of the dark matter around us?
What of the
moments?

In full refusal to admit
that Recall is mere biology,
the mementos speak
as breeze,
as essence.
They fire in her genres
making stone from hint.
Such.

SWIM AWAY
Gilda Griffith Brown

Holding her fishing pole against her left shoulder, the old woman laboriously made her way along the edge of the woods. The path had changed little in a decade, except to grow up snaky. Walking along with a stiff, slow gait, she thought it hadn't seemed that long since her last time fishing. She may have looked as if she was praying with her snow-colored head bent low, but she was on the lookout for a water moccasin or, worse yet, some old copperhead "bad boy."

Though it was early, her feet and ankles were already swollen, and she was out of breath. Stopping for a moment to rest, she thought she heard a rustling sound in the weeds. Raising her head to listen for a moment, she smiled. "It's just a little old jack rabbit, Ella," she scolded herself for her scary imaginings. "He has to move around a bit, too."

"Right so, I reckon he does."

Before continuing on her way, she shifted the canvas bag that hung from her right shoulder in order to ease the pain caused by the thin, cutting straps.

Remembering her last trip along here, she laughed and reminded herself that she had almost run like some young girl. "Ten years makes a lot of difference toward the end of things," she said.

"It does that, all right. Age catches up with a person before they know it," she replied.

Ella Honeywood had been talking to herself for some time. She thought nothing of a two-way conversation, though some would have thought her a crazy old woman. She had come to believe that more old men and old women did it than would be willing to say. Loneliness, more than anything, was the reason, and there was a world full of lonely, old people, she reckoned. "Everyone has to say something sometime," had been her answer to her daughter, Margo, when she caught her doing it a while back. At the time, it got away with Ella, but she didn't pay it any mind now. Her conversations with herself had become a habit that she was content to live with since she had been guilty of worse habits in her lifetime. Besides, she thought, why shouldn't she? After all, she knew herself pretty well after all these years.

She passed the old bent oak tree, older than anyone living, she thought, older than me. She had played under it as a small child while her mama and daddy worked the field. That was only for a short time because she was soon enough put to work beside them. Muttering to herself that it had been a long time ago, she stepped up her pace. Her memories weren't just of them, but they were also of the hot Mississippi sun and the endless days that it had beat upon them. A tireless ball of Southland fire, it penetrated their entire beings, including their good sense. Her mama, when explaining its effect, had often said that after a few hours, the mind could only think of the next weed or cotton boll.

Ella blinked her eyes, blue eyes that looked out from a face that was now pale from inside living. "Don't go and start crying like some baby or ninny," she confronted herself. She could think of no quick-witted retort to make in reply. She only knew that she would not hesitate to step into some kind of time machine and go back there, if she could.

Topping a small rise, Ella swayed and staggered to a stop so that she could get her first look at the pond and its weed-covered bank. Her eyes widened to see it in the clearing. It was as weed and brier free as when she had last seen it.

Nearing the bank, she saw a figure wearing a pink hat sitting across the water from her. The face looked shiny black in the morning sunlight, but Ella couldn't see to make out much else.

She eased her creaky, crying-out bones down to the ground, while hoping at the same time that she'd be able to get back up when the time came. Stretching out on her back, she closed her eyes. The tiredness seemed to roll over her with a flattening effect, but before she went to sleep, she heard herself say, "Get up old woman! That person over there may be a killer."

"I don't care," she answered herself, before slipping away into oblivion.

The harsh caw of a crow flying overhead startled Ella into wakefulness. Looking up at the early September sky, she remained supine and listened for a moment before realizing her whereabouts and remembering the presence across the way. She sat up fast, too fast. Her dizzy gaze could just make out the pink hat that was still across the pond, so she stayed seated there for a spell before pushing herself slowly to her feet.

Taking the jar of worms from her bag, she baited her hook before swinging her line out into the water. She looked across the pond, but the pink hat didn't seem to even notice her. "I guess that person is responsible for the clearing off around my pond," Ella observed, before announcing, "I wouldn't notice me either if I were poaching my fish!"

"Shut up, old woman! Why shouldn't someone else enjoy fishing for bass in your old pond? You sure haven't been making much use of it."

"Well, at least they could have asked."

"Just be thankful that this person is not a killer. While you're about it, you can also be thankful that he or she cleared the weeds and briers away so that you could drag your old self up to the bank and fish one more time before you die."

"I guess that's right." Ella shrugged, as she ended the dialogue.

The only bad thing about arguing with yourself was that you couldn't ever win an argument. She smiled at the thought.

Rested from her nap, she was now more able to enjoy the sights and sounds of life going on all around. Everything was still green, though there would soon be a touch of orange and brown, as autumn began its yearly visit. The earth's "golden days" was how she had always thought of the fall.

Sounds were all around her. She began to name a few in her head: the occasional soft ripple of water, cricket chirps, and a mockingbird song. She could even still hear that old rude crow from time to time.

"You've got a nibble on your line, Ella!"

"Oops! So I have."

"The cork float has gone under! You've got one!"

"Be quiet! I've got things under control."

Minutes later, Ella looked at the little fish that she had just removed from her line. "That old breakfast worm could have cost you big, fishy boy," she informed her catch before throwing him back into the pond. "Swim away, little fish, I don't eat minor leaguers. I'm looking for a big fish."

Glancing around, Ella noticed that the pink hat seemed to be getting nearer all the time. Before long, she got a good look at its wearer. She was a black woman, maybe ten years her junior with thin wiry arms and a gentle face that was worn from living. Ella stared at her for a full minute while she stared right back. They spoke not a word before turning again, each to their own fishing pursuit.

Ten minutes later, with not a lot of yards separating the women, Ella's cork went under again. It was a fight from the beginning, and she realized that she had hooked no average-sized fish. She wasn't sure that she even had the strength to bring it in, but she was too stubborn to give up the fight.

Moments later, surprised and happy that she had been able to bring the big bass in without him breaking her pole, she soon realized that he had been in the pond for some time to have grown so big.

As she began to remove the hook from his mouth, Ella heard talking and turned her head to see that her fishing neighbor had moved even closer. She was smiling widely and gazing at the big bass.

"Do you see that fish she caught?" she asked herself.

"Yeah, I see it, all right. You'd better get busy, old Lucy, and catch you one," she answered her own question.

With wide knowing eyes, Ella looked at her friend and then back at the big old bass that had fought so hard for its survival. "I'd be willing to bet that you'd talk to yourself, too, if you could," she told the fish, before dropping him back into the water.

As Ella watched his dark form swim away and make a lightning dive from sight, she laughed aloud with pure joy. "Swim away, old fish," she said. "We're all kindred spirits here."

"Are you crazy, old woman?" she asked herself.

"Of course, I am. Why do you even ask?"

"She sure is," chimed in a puzzled and surprised Lucy.

CRAZY QUILT
Jane K. Kretschmann

L ying in the back of my closet,
 stained past redemption,
her quilt bears proof of an eye for color,

a steady hand—tiny stitches exact
as a catechism—and a frugal soul,
combining feed sack with fine fabric.

The quilt tells Grandma Clara's last story.
One turbulent spring Sunday,
her eyes wide and wild, Clara

chased her husband from the house,
screaming that she would kill him.
Only her eighth-month belly

prevented Papa from striking her.
As storm clouds roiled blue-black,
green like a bruise,

the children hid in the smokehouse
while Ruth, the oldest,
ran through fields to the nearest friend,

Samuel, part-Creek, part-Negro,
and demanded his help, again.
Samuel grabbed an old quilt

that he used to bring Clara down,
stumbling, her strong white limbs
tangling with his copper ones

like a beast from Revelation.
After the storm, the sheriff
wrapped Clara in the quilt—

its red and purple patchwork
a bright foil for her haunted face—
and took her to an asylum in Tuscaloosa.

There Clara delivered her child, stillborn.
For three more years her moans
were lullaby to her empty arms.

TICK ATTACK IN TENNESSEE
Susie Dunham

Not long ago, my husband, Bossman, and I ventured off in our Winnebago to check out retirement property in central Tennessee.

We thought we were looking for land in all the right places as we explored beautiful properties with views of golf courses, mountains, and lakes. Heavily wooded acres nourished pines, hardwood trees, prickly bushes, burr-like grasses, and stealth-like bugs.

Giant moss-draped boulders dotted the hills. We were awestruck by the pristine nature we tripped through and fell over. Rocks, acorns, pine needles, and oak leaves occasionally nestled a stray golf ball. We found six. "Good ones," according to my golfer guy. They were pocketed as rewards for our vigorous exercise.

Hidden within the forest, a beautiful golf course jumped over meandering streams and stood its ground against miles of newly paved roads. New homes will be constructed in these woods and along this golf course. The many deer and small furry animals we saw as we tromped over their trails and huts will soon play chicken with predicted traffic that will run the roads to numerous golf courses and bountiful banks.

The street we parked on was deserted. The area we walked through was homeless.

After we finished our amateur surveying, golf ball picking, and "Oh my God, look at that view!" saying, we trudged back to the Jeep. As we climbed in and prepared to leave, I looked at Bossman and noticed a weird little bug on his forearm. I leaned in closer.

"Uh oh. It's a tick!" I plucked it off his arm and dropped it out the window.

"Hey," he said, "You've got one, too," and picked it off my shoulder.

It's a widely known fact that ticks travel in herds.

We jumped from the Jeep, met each other at the tailgate, and looked down each other's shirts like middle-schoolers. Only it wasn't for thrills—it was for ticks, and we were loaded with them. I tried frantically to get the snaps undone on my blouse, as Bossman struggled to get his golf shirt pulled over his head. The trick was not to bring any ticks along for the ride that might drop into his eyes, run up his nose, or parachute into his hair.

Finally stripped down to my Eighteen-Hour, I jumped around, waved my blouse like a flag of surrender, and spouted a lot of "Oh my Gods" while trying to pick ticks off my chest.

Bossman, shirtless, tried to keep me still so he could pick bugs off my back.

"Oh boy, that one was really digging in."

I didn't need to know that and started to hop around again.

Now it was my turn to check Bossman's upper body. I removed ticks from his back and chest and felt one with the apes.

"Check your waistband!" Bossman said as he peeked into his. We both pulled at our jeans and saw those nasty ticks moving south. We dropped our Levi's, and they pooled around our ankles. Bossman's ticks marched through his forest-like legs with the exception of one who got attached to his inner thigh. Who could blame it? I pulled that little bugger out and felt good about it.

"Good grief, they're in my underwear!" I yelled as I looked where few men have dared to tread. But that's another story.

Bossman scuffed his way up to the front of the Jeep to have some privacy behind the open driver's door as he peeked to make sure they hadn't invaded his Jockeys. Again, who could blame them? Thank goodness no one was house hunting on the road we were playing half-naked-monkey-doctor on. We inspected our sneakers, socks, jeans, and shirts before we got back into the Jeep. We were spent. Exhausted. No more traipsing through the woods like little storybook characters for us.

What did Red Riding Hood do when she got ticks? What about Goldilocks and those bears who had to have carried those nasty little buggers? How did they survive those savage bloodsuckers? I had a new respect for those Grimm creations.

Once back in the privacy of our motorhome, we thought it best to examine ourselves again. Down came the shades and off came the clothes. Oh, no! More ticks.

Plucky enough to follow us home, they had turned into stalker ticks. We showed no mercy and pinched them till they popped.

Bossman, flashlight in hand, performed a husbandly body search on me. Such intimacy can only be shared by a couple with ticks. We've been married over thirty years, and we've never been closer. Trust me on that.

We shook our clothes and put them into plastic garbage bags. Then we took steaming hot showers. Dressed in fresh clothes, we still had the creepy crawlies.

The next day we discussed retiring in a tick-free zone. We talked about the bug invasion and agreed we would have missed out on quite a story if we'd run into bunnies instead.

Little did we know the story wasn't over. Back home, two days after the tick attack, as I was drying off from my shower, I felt a small raised dot on my left hip. Not having my glasses on, I picked at it and placed it on the bathroom sink. It looked round, brown, familiar, and blurred.

I returned less than a minute later wearing my glasses.

It was gone.

THE ROOM
Kathleen Vibbert

The room has no temper.
  All the red is gone,
the doilies my mother embroidered
never served a purpose.
They came and went, white on white.

Eyes fed into lace,
thin tails reminding
me of her fingers.
I'd like the amaryllis
on the coffee table,
drapes tucked back
into their armpits,
the sun swaggering through.

It shouldn't be in solitary,
the moths covered in plastic.
Straw-rooted poppies spindle
into the corners.

I long for her magnolias,
threads that bear fruit,
and bulbs diverged
along the looping vine.

THE GRAVE DIGGER
Louise Colln

A small terrapin, exposed at the road's hot center to an earthshaking roar, stretched its neck and pumped its legs till it tumbled into a dust-lined rut and closed its shell. Roy Crouch didn't feel the crunch as pieces of its shell flew into the dust cloud his rattling Model-T truck flung behind him. He wouldn't have been concerned if he had. Terrapins weren't one of the things the sun-dried hills of Eastern Oklahoma were short of in 1931.

He was concerned with the small, round woman who sat beside him. The folds of her print-clad body bounced gently as her weathered face peered out at him indignantly from under the ruffle of her sunbonnet.

"You'd do that, Roy? Disturb the dead for money?"

"Course I would, Leeth. It ain't like they died recent, or's anybody we know. They ain't nothin' but old Indian bones."

"Indians are people. We've always welcomed Indians into our house, same's whites."

"Never said they wasn't people. And I'd dig a grave for Indians just as quick as for whites. Done it before, out on the hill in our own graveyard, with our own dead. But these here Indians, they've been dead for hundreds, maybe thousands of years. Don't seem like real people anymore. Savages, they was then."

"Savages that could find something you can't now. Gold, maybe jewels, to hear you talk."

"Don't have to be gold, Leeth. There's fellers over in Fort Smith willing to buy anything from them graves. Even flat rocks or mussel shells they've cut pictures into. All I have to do is help Jake dig into them mounds the old savages built up down by the river."

"You always said you respected them. Felt a kinship with them, from the kind of work you do."

"Do respect them. Them old boys, they knew how to build a grave."

He twisted the truck into the weedy ruts of his driveway and stopped it with a bone-shaking grind of brakes, then looked at Leeth apprehensively.

"Seems like you've lost more weight," he said, squeezing the too-soft flesh of her thigh. He thought wistfully of how, just a few months ago, it was so solid it pushed back against his hand, tight against her dress.

"Now don't you go complaining about my legs," she said, shoving his hand away playfully. "There's still plenty of me for the likes of you."

"You coughed blood again last night, didn't you?"

He swung himself down and followed her through the heat-crisped grass to the small, weather-silvered, clapboard house.

She pushed through the patched screen door without answering, letting it slam behind her without watching that it didn't hit him. For a minute he stood outside it, looking around. Everything in his sight was run down and dead looking. One old cow stood up to her bag in a muddy pond beside the small barn. Chickens pecked sluggishly through the bare barnyard outside a pen where a skinny gilt pig lay in the dust.

He turned away and followed her in. She stood at the wooden kitchen table, staring at nothing. She jerked around when she heard the door shut and tried to pretend she was rubbing at a stain on the cloth-polished wood. Roy knew that stain had been there for years, and Leeth had given up trying to get it off. She would've had it off long ago, the way she was always washing and dusting their three-room house. Even the old kitchen range shone clean in its blackness.

He looked into the sitting room where the twin rockers that his mother had left them stood. Leeth's care for thirty years had kept their swirling indentations softly shimmering. He couldn't see beyond to their bedroom, but he could feel, as a part of his body, the many years of sweet and happy nights between apple-smelling, sun-dried sheets.

"I'd go face-to-face with them old grave diggers if it'd get us enough for you to go to Memphis to a good hospital where they'd do something about whatever is taking you over." He went back to their conversation without explanation, knowing she would follow his thinking. "Some do say if we'd find where the chief's buried, we'd find gold. Enough we'd just walk into some good doctor and say, 'Money's no object, Doc. Just make her well.' Way the rich guys in those stories you read do."

He rubbed his hand against the stained table, not quite touching hers.

"Roy." She swung around to face him. "If I'm going to get well, I'll get well. And a grave is a grave, and it's a sin not to give it respect. I don't want to live with the ghost of an Indian chief because we stole the things his people put in to honor him. Let him be, Roy."

He eyed her stubbornly without answering. He knew when she turned away and picked up her knife to start peeling potatoes that she'd read his silence. He was going to dig.

He and Jake Pierce worked together. Roy digging, using his fine feel for forming a neat grave to slide his shovel into the long mounds without breaking anything. Jake washed the pieces of pottery and shells they found and carried them across the river to Fort Smith where someone bought them for his own collection or for a museum where they didn't much care how they got their specimens. Roy didn't ask. He'd fight the devil hand-to-hand for whatever was buried if it would buy Leeth's life.

At first he felt ridges running through his hair when he stuck his shovel into the grass-and-weed-covered hillocks, his mind pulling up a vision of copper-skinned people carrying their treasures in to bury with a stiffened body meant to rest forever under the baskets of dirt they threw over it. But after a while, he stopped thinking of them. He dug quickly, then went on to another spot, not taking time to open all the way to the bottom anywhere, for fear someone else might find the old chief's mound.

Old Chief. Old Chief was hiding the big stuff that would mend Leeth's body for him. Every time he stuck his shovel into a new part of a mound, he prayed fiercely that this one would be Old Chief's grave, prickly with gold and jewels.

He learned to meet Leeth's eyes without shame when he came home at night, only feeling sorrow that they weren't finding anything big. It was too obvious that something had to be done soon. Every day she grew weaker, coughed up more blood that she tried to hide from him.

The next time they had enough to sell, he got the name of the man who was buying from Jake. He took the specimens across the river himself and did some horse-trading. The man agreed to send Leeth to a hospital in Memphis if Roy promised to bring everything he dug up to him. Even then Roy didn't mention Old Chief's jewels.

They made the trip to Memphis in his old truck, though he worried that it would be too hard for Leeth. But she sat quietly beside him, not reminding him that she still thought what he was doing was wrong.

They were good to her at the hospital. A doctor examined her thoroughly and made x-ray pictures of her chest. Then he sat down beside Leeth's bed in the drab-smelling ward and spoke honestly. "I can't help you. I'm sorry. There's so much we don't know how to cure yet. Tuberculosis. Maybe if you could get out to Arizona, it might be longer, but . . ."

Reading the hopelessness in their eyes, he left them.

"Arizona. If I can find Old Chief's grave."

"Don't, Roy. Leave him in peace, like I'd want to be left. I'm not one to run from death, Roy. I know there's a heaven waiting."

"There's a hell for me if you die. What if I don't find you again? What if I don't make it to your heaven? Or you're hid from me in some better part of it than I'll ever earn? Like that Old Chief's hiding from me. But I'll find him. Just you see."

"Seems like it's turned into a game, Roy. He's the hider, you're the seeker."

"I'll find him. I'll take you to Arizona."

"I don't think you hear me anymore, Roy. You and the chief. That's all you hear. What's going on in your mind?"

"I'll find him, soon's we get you out of here and get back to Oklahoma."

But Leeth didn't leave the hospital. When they called him to her deathbed in the night, too late for good-bye, he wondered if in some unknown way she had willed it. To keep him from dogging Old Chief till he found him and used his grave treasures to try and hold her.

Her body rode back across Arkansas in the back of his truck, lying in a cheap casket the hospital people had helped him get. He drove carefully over the roads, not to shake her too much. He let the driving keep him from thinking or feeling.

Neighbors came over, carrying food, like he'd ever feel like eating again. They offered to dig her grave, even though he was the only one who ever stuck spade into their hillside cemetery. They blared their eyes in some kind of judgment when he refused the offer, but he didn't care. Nothing but the best was good enough for Leeth, and everyone knew he was the best. He went alone to open the ground for her.

Long ago, when he'd first started digging graves, he'd claimed the top of the hill for him and Leeth. It was a long way up from the dirt road where he'd parked his truck, and the two shovels weighed him down as though he were carrying the load of Leeth's empty body.

He pushed past the old graves, ones dug by someone else before he was born, and ones he'd dug, himself. The inhabitant of each grave seemed to rise up and stand before him as he walked past. Old Sam Evans who'd lived beyond what anyone had any right to expect and wore out his relatives in doing it. Young Sam, his great grandson, who'd got hit with a piling on a railroad gang, and years before his time, warmed the ground for the old man. Seemed like when there was push and shove between bad and good, bad always won. People like Leeth died.

He walked the perimeter of the grave, judging the dimensions in his mind, as he marked the edges with the point of his shovel. Then he set to work, hauling out big shovelfulls of damp clayey earth with every coordinated drive of his legs and arms. He placed the dirt carefully in a small hillock beside the grave so it would be easy for someone to shovel it back in. Someone else. He couldn't throw dirt on top of Leeth. It'd take all his strength just to walk back down that hill, leaving her here.

He was down almost to the bottom of the grave, down where it was always just him and the earth about him, when something fell through the sidewall and hit his shovel with a soft click. He knelt down, sifting through the loosened dirt toward a glimmer of white bones. An unmarked grave, here where he wanted to rest with just Leeth near him. None of *his* digging. Someone else before his time had left a body here. Well, he'd just wall the bones back up again. Leeth was always a friendly one. She'd gladly share her ground.

He gathered up the finger bones. Almost a whole hand. A man's hand. Tall, probably. The bones were long. He opened up a bigger hole in the wall of Leeth's grave to slip the bones back in to be with the rest of the stranger's body, and with a dry rattle, a handful of pearls fell through.

Roy picked one up. It was brown with age and packed-on dirt. Worthless. He cradled it in his hand, not thinking of the worth of pearls. Those old Indians, they buried their chiefs on a bed of freshwater pearls, torn from the mussel shells in the river.

Their chiefs! Even as he stood there, alone in Leeth's grave, more pearls sifted through. He knelt and slipped his hand into the other grave. He touched a bone and a wide band. A bracelet most likely. Probably beaten copper. Maybe gold. There'd likely be a breastplate, too. Maybe a metal facemask.

He stretched up so his eyes came just above the rim of Leeth's grave, needing to see light. Why hadn't he thought of it before? Of course, the chief would be buried at the top of the highest hill around. Beside the river. Probably half the dirt on the hill had been basketed up from the riverbank. Dirt he'd been shoveling all these years, packed down by all the time and weather gone by.

So here he was. Old Chief in his game of hide-and-seek. He'd played a good game, hiding in Roy's own graveyard. Now Roy'd found him.

"E-E-E-I," he yelled in imitation of his lost childhood voice. "I found Chiefie, hiding in the graveyard." Scaring himself, yelling out here, all alone in Leeth's grave.

But Old Chief had won the game anyhow, Roy knew. He should have yelled, "Allee, allee, all in free."

All he had left was regret that Leeth had died feeling like he'd gone away from her, had lost himself in a game with a dead Indian. All that Old Chief meant to him now was time away from Leeth when she was still alive. Times he'd left her even while he'd lain in bed beside her. He felt the bitterness rise up inside him. What good was gold, old pearls, to him now?

So now Leeth, who'd never wanted the chief disturbed, would rest beside him, guarding him with her own body. Roy knew he'd never tell anyone that he had finally found the prize. That would mean that Leeth would be disturbed.

But he'd know that she lay beside gold and precious stones just like the Bible said she'd walk among in heaven. Or was it pearls she was worth on earth? He knew that for sure. But he'd honor her. He wouldn't take out even the pearls or the bracelet he'd felt on Old Chief's wrist bone. Let Leeth and Old Chief rest among the riches, and someday he'd join them. Help her guard him.

Working carefully, he placed Old Chief's hand bones back through the hole in the side of Leeth's grave. Back beside the rest of the body he knew was in there. He shoved the pearls through with them.

And then, without willing his hand to move, he felt the bracelet again with one finger. Surely after chasing Old Chief all this time, after giving up so much of Leeth's last days, he'd bought and paid for something.

He could tell the bracelet was loose, probably fell off the end of the arm when the hand and pearls fell out. He hooked his finger around the circlet and pulled it out. It was greenish with time and dirt, but heavy. He didn't know enough about metals to identify it. He'd seen precious little gold in his lifetime.

He walled up the grave with the clayey dirt, and climbed out. He walked over to the riverbank, carrying the bracelet.

He stood for a long time, watching a snake cross the river. It was a big one, swimming strongly, its thick body curving masterfully within the vee of water it pushed up with its head.

Roy envied it. It knew where it was going. Didn't worry about why. Just using all its strength to get there.

Like him. Like he'd done. Never questioning the sense of doing it. But that's what a man had to do if he's going after something with everything he has inside.

He'd used all his strength looking for Old Chief and his treasure, hoping it would let him hold onto Leeth a little longer. He'd got so deep in finding the chief that he'd let him become more real than the truth he couldn't accept. He couldn't keep Leeth from dying.

Something inside him hoped that Leeth understood, that though he'd lost precious time with her, he'd done all he could the only way he knew how. He'd shoved his whole self against the current of the little time they had left, the way that snake had shoved itself against the current of the river.

Hoped? He knew she understood. Leeth wouldn't fault him now. She'd be glad for him that he'd finally found the treasure for her without bothering Old Chief's rest.

For her.

He walked back to the grave and let himself down in it, careful to not disturb its sharp edges. At the bottom he dug a little hole, deep enough that no one would catch any glint of color or shine. He slipped the bracelet into the hole and covered it, to lie under her body until the judgment trump rang out and they all stepped up from the ground, maybe holding hands with Old Chief.

"Told you I'd win the game, Leeth. Found the old boy, didn't I?"

He climbed out of the grave.

"I'll find you too, Leeth. I'll find you again."

SWEET HOME ALABAMA
Kathleen Vibbert

I 'll write till summer ends,
my thumbs calloused,
dipped in chocolate mint.
Yellow fog approaches my narratives—
to crouch and slowly finger
my outer extremities.
I'll float in the lake,
until my hair is a fan—
gray plumes braided into tiny whores.
People who gather around my tomb
will whisper
"She was such a wonderful person."
I'll be safe inside
this charming place,
humming
Sweet Home Alabama
while the crows outside steal my seed.

TENNESSEE SEASONS
S. R. Lee

W *inter Day*

Drawn together by difficulties,
not so unusual,
cold, damp, age, dusk,
the dog and two humans
stay near the fire
companionably.

Quick Snow

Quick, quick snow
speeding downwards,
small bits
take time to cover ground,
are not clinging to trees,
not even cedars.
The air is gray
between here and hills
because quick, quick snow
is speeding downwards.

Winter Sun

Winter sun, mornings,
heat unexpected,
even with west wind stinging,
a thread of heat
felt on shoulders
turned eastward.

Sun heat, small stranger
above frost-white grass, ice-hard earth,
wind-pushed branches semaphoring "cold, cold, cold."

Winter sun reaches
through galactic spaces to
earth's winter chill
to say "Survive."

Winter sun, afternoons,
low to southwest,
horizontal streaks flare through windows.
Field animals stand broadside to sunlight,
pleased with one warm side.

The morning stranger has become clearly present,
west-moving commuters squint
as well as those who,
working or sporting outside,
brave the winter air.

Sun pushing, shoving,
enticing us with light,
Cold will not overcome.
Although distant,
sometimes hidden,
sun never leaves.

January Daffodils

'determined,
   brief lives
bright,

warmth encouraged
   sprout
then chill wind, snow.

they flower
   sun-colored
in the cold.

Wild Onions

Hello, wild onions,
edible but bitter
bane of those who milk cows,
leaping up in tufts
   across the lawn,

among the trees.
You bring the same news of spring
   as early daffodils.

Opening Culverts in the Rain

Sturdy oak leaves
Crouch in sodden dark,
Their obstructive task
Aided by sticks caught crookedly
In the concrete pipe.

Water pouring
Swiftly down the hillside
Ignores barriers
And runs wild, spreading,
Pooling, cutting new gullies.
Debris-filled streams
Cross roads, cut through fields,
Bring neighborhood flotsam.
Dead grass, paper bits,
Plastic bottles, armfuls of straw
Swirl and rush everywhere along with
Water pounding from sky
To land, from hilltop to creekbed.

With hoe and fox shovel, a man walks
Bent despite raincoat and hood,
Displaced water soaking his shoes.
He probes, pushes, shovels, scrapes.

A stick loosened, muddy water
Spouts from the culvert end.
Leaves scraped from a grate,
The growing lake in the drive becomes shallow.
Some judiciously removed mud
Makes way for water swift
To flow toward the creek,
Less then spilling into the pastures.

Wet and bone tired, he goes to the house
For a cup of coffee, removes muddy shoes
Outside, strips off wet socks
In the bathroom, refuses his wife's
Hovering condolences, and settles to
The five-fifteen weather report.

Into Summer

Green joy of June beginning
warms slowly toward a threat of dry
earth. Ripening requires heat,
warmth, but warm encourages slow wilt
everywhere.

Hay browns in fields.
Streams are shallowing.
Flowers suffer the late day's sun,
await their nightly sprinkling.
Squirrels seeking water
drown in the horse trough.

Rain, descend on us.
Plants, flourish for us.
Green, stay with us.

Summer Dark

At the edge of the yard,
Small sounds bombard
The black air. Cicadas, tree frogs
Clinging to bark,
Rasp their mating calls
On and on and on. Among these,
A faint screech drops intermittently,
Perhaps beyond the barn,
So distant one's not sure
What. A young owl?

As evening cools, the air
Stirs, swirls between trees, softly
Pushes leaves, tall grasses,
Where, feeling safer from hawk
Or cat, small ones run so lightly
Through the undergrowth no paw patters
Reach my casual human ear.
The owl, or some other nocturnal being,
May be sharper. Beware! Take Care!

No moon, scattered clouds
Allow but dim star-shine,
Not a night to walk across the fields.

Instead sit still, do not go stumbling,
For there is no need.

So I, worn with the day's frets,
Sit silent, breathe slowly,
With little thought.
What urgencies are in the dark,
What love songs or hunger-searches,
Hardly register. My swaying mind
Dreams in fragments of the past.
The dark night air like
The brain's huge unconscious,
Is filled with glories and horrors,
But in this summer darkness
Night brushes me lightly.

Fragment of Creation

A small white skull
   among dead leaves
  at first looked like trash,
    a ball of paper perhaps?
    something dirty?
No, not trash.

It had a different death from that of leaves,
   for its life was longer and more needy,
 a series of events
    as the little hunter slipped through the underbrush
      seeking and avoiding,

attracting its kind,
fearing the owl
and dogs.

Finally something happened, so the creature died
  and lay among dead leaves.
        partially eaten?
        rotting quickly in the summer's heat?

Stripped of flesh and skin,
  the bones separate, scatter,
  except that a skull has no joints,
      is a single unit.
          Alone it bleaches
            paler, paler,
      until among the dead leaves,
          dry, brittle, thin, white,
      it attracts, is lifted,
        the eye holes and long nose bone noted.

It could have been smashed under a shoe,
    but no,
        it still lies among the dead leaves.

UNFULFILLED
Currie Alexander Powers

C airo trotted into the woods feeling the warmth of the sun leave her back as she moved into the cool darkness of the trees. The skin on her belly felt loose and papery and swayed from side to side as she moved. The weight of her nipples fought with gravity. She only had a few moments, feeling the other pull. Not gravity—the tug of duty.

A squirrel darted across her path and she froze. It flicked its tail and opened its mouth, emitting an angry trill, then fled up a tree trunk. Cairo felt her heart beat with an excitement she'd forgotten. For months now, her heart beat only for them, first in her belly, then curled into her side, small, shivering, dependent. She contemplated going after the squirrel, but there were better things to pursue.

This morning Cairo had remembered the tall spruce tree with the skirt of low branches. She remembered rolling beneath it, then running fast and strong, her body tight and weightless. She remembered being one. Now she was many.

Her back quivered. Maybe it was time to return to the shed. She turned her head and looked at the opening of sunlight back in the trees. A rustling on the ground startled her and she spun around. Her ears curled forward, listening. There, she heard it, a rustle, followed by a faint whimper.

Her nose lifted, scanning the air. Another muffled whimper. She took three steps forward, eyeing a dark patch under the skirt of the spruce, the hair on her back stiffening. Something white moved and she heard a dry choked cry. Cairo's heart seized, and an ache started in her nipples. No, she couldn't have. She couldn't have forgotten one. She plunged forward under the branches and caught the smell, the rusty odor of dried blood.

The white covering was cool in her mouth, but she felt the warm softness underneath as she pulled it clear of the branches. It rolled with her, heavy and pliant, coming to a stop on top of her front feet. Cairo nosed the opening of the bag, and the smell of birth surrounded her; a sound bubbled in her throat. She sniffed the hair on the head, then tasted the wetness. It was salty and sweet and Cairo remembered it. She pawed the opening of the white bag, exposing the large head, then stopped and stood back, unsure of the smooth hairless body. It was very pink, streaked with blood, and the front legs were jerking, little rolls of fat creased at the joints. Cairo examined the strange divided digits that curled and straightened, clutching the air. It was so much larger than the others. Cairo looked at the eyes and mouth. They looked similar, the eyes squeezed into folds, the mouth bunched and wet, making sucking sounds.

Her heart was beating with urgency and confusion. She didn't remember squeezing out this one under the tree. She remembered the rest, one after the other, sliding out from between her legs into the soft blanket in the box that the tall, thin man made for her in the shed. He'd been there, stroking her head, his soft voice soothing her over the pain. She remembered the pain. It had started in the morning as she walked heavily through the woods. Then it had taken over and she didn't remember going back to the shed, only that something had guided her there. Maybe she'd been distracted by the pain, had stopped here and let the large one come, then accidentally left it behind.

Cairo licked the large pink head and nosed the warm cheek. It made a cooing sound and jerked a front leg, hitting Cairo's neck. Then the long paws burrowed into her fur and Cairo knew it was hers. The others burrowed their paws in her belly before they sucked her milk. She had to get it back to the shed.

She fit her mouth around the neck, feeling for the loose section of skin. The skin was too tight, and it gave a distressed whimper. Too much time had passed. The pull to go back was growing stronger. Cairo pawed the bag back up over the shoulders and grabbed the loose ends in her teeth. It was heavier than she expected and she tipped over, nose in the dirt, on the first try. Planting her hind legs wider apart, she pulled harder, straining to lift her head and the bundle in her teeth. The pink bundle went still as if knowing not to resist Cairo's efforts. It took a few tries, and Cairo dropped the bundle twice, misjudging the distribution of weight—heavier on the head side than the feet side—but she finally got a good hold and carried it out of the forest.

Crossing the big street with its constant rush of cars was a challenge, and Cairo's heart stopped for a full three seconds when she heard the screech of brakes behind her just as she hopped to safety on the other side. The pink bundle kept quiet. Across the broken pavement of the parking lot, between the two dumpsters around back, over a cracked patch of dirt and grass, through another parking lot, Cairo carried the bundle in her teeth. Her jaws hurt, but the longer she held onto the bundle, the more she possessed it, and if anyone had tried to take it from her, they would have had to pry her jaws loose.

Cairo stopped to rest when she came to the fence. She dropped the bundle at her feet, then stood with her body over it, protecting it from the blunt burning sun. She looked at the fence, panting and anxious. It was made of strings of metal with pointed little spears that caught her fur when she crawled under. Alone it was a tight fit to get on the other side where Cairo could see the shed. She fitted the bundle in her jaws again and went to the spot where the space under the fence was the biggest. She could smell her own scent on the wire as she stuck her nose under the lowest string of metal and inched forward until it rested on her neck. The bundle rolled on the ground and pressed against Cairo's body, wedging her against the strand of metal. Cairo pushed her front legs up, feeling the metal cut across her shoulders, digging into her fur. She pushed harder, raising the string of metal until she could fit herself and the bundle underneath. One of the sharp spears caught her back; she felt the sting as it punctured her skin. She kept pushing under the fence regardless, because her heart was telling her she had no choice but to go forward. The shed was just a short distance away, the pull of its proximity strong, and with a final push she was through with the bundle still in her mouth.

She limped into the shed through the square in the bottom of the door. The tall, thin man had made the hole for her after the others came. A small chorus of squeals rose as Cairo neared the box. Their newborn blindness did not prevent them from sensing the arrival of food and warmth.

Cairo put the bundle down in the box and one of the small ones squealed and squirmed out from under the pink, hairless mammoth. Cairo nosed the loose end of the bag open, freeing the large head, then she crawled into the box, circling to find room in what was now a very crowded space, and then she lay down on her side and waited for the small bodies and the large one to blindly find their way to her nipples. She fell asleep, feeling the sucking pull of little mouths, and at last she relaxed. They were all accounted for.

When the tall, thin man came to bring Cairo's bowl of food, he saw the large hairless one and began making excited noises. He looked at Cairo, questioning sounds accompanying his hand movements. He picked the large hairless one up, pulled the white bag off and threw it aside. Cairo watched him with proud eyes. The man cradled it on its back, staring at the squeezed eyes and the bunched mouth. Then it opened its mouth and let out a wail that went on and on, building, then hiccupping. Cairo got to her feet, dislodging the others, concerned by this new sound. The others didn't sound like that. Cairo went to the man where he knelt, holding the large one over his shoulder now, patting its back and making soothing sounds. She put her nose on the large one's foot, whimpering for the man to put it back in the box, so it would stop the loud wailing. Then the man started to rise to his feet, out of Cairo's reach, and she grabbed the large one's ankle in her mouth, trying to pull him back. The man shook his head, pushing Cairo away, then patted her. Cairo trusted him and sat back on her hind legs. The man looked at her kindly, his voice low and gentle, then he carried the large one away, opening the door to the shed with his shoulder, letting in a moment of brilliant sunshine as the door swung open. Then it shut again, and the shed was shadowed.

Cairo went to the door and sat down in front of it and waited. After a while she crawled through the hole in the bottom of the door and went to the back of the tall, thin man's house and waited by his door. When the sun went away, she went back to the shed and let the remaining ones nuzzle her fur until they fell asleep.

The emptiness grew in her as the hours passed. Even while the others sucked on her and pressed their small warm bodies against her, Cairo felt the absence of the big one. It was like an unclaimed territory existed right next to her, wide and incomplete.

Cairo's heart beat slow and hard. And when the tall, thin man returned the next day and the next, his arms empty, even though Cairo knew the province of motherhood with the others, she also knew what it was to be unfulfilled, and she mourned the one she'd rescued under the trees.

Oriel moaned in her sleep, her hand going to her belly. It felt hard and unforgiving and when she went to roll on her back, the weight of her stomach rolled her back on her side. She drew her knees up and tried to find her dreams again. She was running fast and strong, her body tight and weightless. The woods of her childhood, the quiet burrow under the big spruce tree, the low skirt of branches hiding her from the limitations of her family. They had limits for everything—tolerance, patience, and love. In her fifteen years, Oriel had learned that the trees in the woods were more forgiving than her parents. They welcomed her with their open branches and let her climb into their arms. They were her comfort and joy until she met the young boy. He was sixteen. He had loved her. And now he was gone. Disappeared, like a ghost.

Oriel's belly had started to grow shortly afterwards, and at first she thought she was swelling with grief, her unshed tears filling her like a bottle that had no opening. She felt sick all the time. Her breasts grew large and tender, lined with dark veins, and when she lay under the spruce tree in the spot she and the boy had lain together, she touched her mutating body and suddenly knew. The ghost boy had left something behind.

Oriel hid her growing body from her parents. She wore shawls, told them she was cold, and spent as much time in the woods as she could. When her belly was too large to hide, she ran away and made a bed for herself under the skirt of the spruce and waited to be released.

The ache went on for two days. When it was over, Oriel felt a different ache, the ache of emptiness.

When she heard the voices calling her name deep in the forest, she realized they were looking for her. She hid the sleeping bundle in a bag for warmth and crawled out from under the tree. Her aunt found her, and when she saw her bloodstained skirt, she wrapped her shawl around Oriel and put her finger to her lips, mouthing the word *secret*. Then the aunt called to the others.

The next morning, Oriel was handed over to the man her parents had selected for her to marry. He was ten years older and sleepy eyed. He gave Oriel's father a gold bowl. As he prepared to lead Oriel away, she caught the eye of her aunt and mouthed, *secret?* Her aunt looked away.

Oriel's husband took her far away. Too far for her to

make her way back to the woods. A year after they were married, they still had no children. Five years later, her husband shrugged and gave up.

The emptiness grew in Oriel as each day passed. Though she knew the province of marriage, she also knew what it was to be unfulfilled, and she mourned the boy who had loved her and what they'd left behind under the trees.

Tekra was seven when the tall, thin man came back to the orphanage for him. He was past the age that a family would want him, and they'd contacted the tall, thin man, asking if he wanted to take him. They'd been kind to Tekra at the orphanage, and he'd been useful, helping them take care of the babies, though just as Tekra would form a bond with one, it was taken away. He'd grown accustomed to the empty feeling inside, the nagging pull to curl up with others, and he'd come to think of it like gravity, a force he couldn't fight.

The tall, thin man smiled a lot and had expressive blue eyes. He took Tekra to his house and while Tekra ate, the man hovered over him as though anxious to please. Through the window Tekra could see a shed in the backyard with a hole cut in the bottom of the door. A long, brown nose stuck out of the hole, and Tekra watched as first one, then another, then another, soft brown and tan dog shimmied out and ran across the yard to the back door. He could hear the wet push of their breath against the door and the scrape of their nails on the concrete step. Tekra got up from the table, and the tall, thin man followed him out into the yard, where the swarm of brown and tan dogs circled Tekra, pressing their bodies against him. He laughed and sat down, letting them step on his legs and arms with the large black pads of their feet. He put his face in their fur, and the smell filled him up. The tall, thin man was smiling so hard now, he was squeezing the moisture out of his face, and it ran down his cheeks and curled under his jaw into the collar of his shirt. The brown and tan dogs formed a circle around Tekra and settled in the dirt with him, panting, their tongues loose, occasionally tipping their heads up, making soft 'ruffs' and nosing his face.

The tall, thin man left Tekra in the yard with the dogs while he went to the market. He looked back at Tekra as he was closing the gate, shaking his head and smiling.

After a while, the dogs got up and went to the shed. Tekra followed them, opening the door into the darkness, waiting a moment till he could see into the shadows. There was a boxed-off area made of low wood walls. It was large enough for all the dogs, and inside there was an old blue blanket on a bed of straw. Tekra didn't see the other dog until she lifted her head and gave a soft questioning bark. Tekra could see by the tufts of gray fur that she was older than the other dogs. He approached slowly, watching her dark eyes. She was regarding him carefully, but urging him to come closer. Tekra knelt in the box and held out his hand for her to smell.

Her nose was cold against his fingers, and she inhaled his scent rapidly, then stopped suddenly. She didn't snap or grab him, but her mouth closed around his wrist and she tugged him forward. Tekra moved closer to her side. She didn't let go of his wrist until he lay against her shoulder. Her head came around, sniffing his hair, his forehead. She nudged his head forward, sniffing around back, and then Tekra felt her mouth close around the back of his neck. He went still, anxious for a moment that she meant to bite him. Her lips moved on his nape, then her teeth very gently pulled at his skin, tugging him toward her. Tekra shifted closer and rested his head on her. She made a low murmur in her throat and let go of his neck.

Cairo laid her head down and sighed. Tekra burrowed his hands in her fur. A moment later the other dogs settled around him. One curled in the hollow of Tekra's knees, another put its head across his hip, another draped itself over his feet.

Tekra closed his eyes, smelling the warm sweetness of Cairo's fur, listening to the sighs of the other dogs, then the chorus of breathing as they all fell asleep. The emptiness inside him vanished, and the pull to be close to others, Tekra's personal gravity, suddenly had a new purpose. Instead of giving in to it, Tekra welcomed it, the press of warm bodies anchoring him to earth.

Cairo felt the cold space beside her warm with life. They were all accounted for.

UPCOUNTRY CAROLINA
HOMECOMING
Louise Colln

Cousins, kissing,
    talk and listen
on parallel tiers,
in acappella roundelay.
Matching syllable to syllable,
they sew words lightly,
soul warming pieces of patchwork quilts
stitched together with hugs.

They discuss ancestors as part of present lives;
"Great-grand-daddy met Great-grand-mama at Seneca,
in nineteen ought four." They dissect dour sepia pictures
for foreheads and lips, lay fingers across chins and noses;
"See that mouth, that's George. There's Great-grand-daddy,
for sure, there in Marshall's eyes."

Conversation boils
like cresting cusps of mountain rivers;
tongues curl richly around native names,
Tugaloo . . . Toccoa . . . Wakulla . . . Walhalla . . . Nantahala . . .
Swannanoa . . . Tuckasegee . . . Keowea;
crooning tones
blend with the shade tree music

of flattop guitar, banjo, fiddle,
clacking spoons, and clogging feet
on squares of wood. Sweet dulcimers sing
above the feathery squeals of playing children.
Mothers smile.

"Honey, just mash that light on for me, where's Grand-
mama, oh, she had to go make a branch, never mind, you
might could put more Ritz crackers in that macaroni and
cheese pie, m-m-m don't that smell good, though?"

Kitchen smells,
biscuits, chicken, ham,
barbecue,
swirl out to gladdened noses,
braiding and unbraiding with scents
of hibiscus, gardenias, purple thrift,
roses, creamy lilies.

Old horseshoe pitchers
under the chinaberry tree
pause and think eagerly
of the feast to come after the blessing.
They laugh about their long childhood wait
for the old-timey preacher
to bless the children,
bless the green grass,
bless the blue sky,
bless the (cooling) food to our (hungry) bodies.
The old men bless the young minister
who sends God a short e-mail
instead of an epistle.

They speak briefly, with lowered lids, of emotional
blessings, of children, of wives. "That grand-son of mine
is a pistol, all right." Then they pick up horseshoes
again, not looking at the one who stands in silence,
remembering grief.

Half-focused on target stakes,
leaners,
ringers,
they listen for the signal
to break bread together with kinfolk;
savor already
respect due and given to the elders of the clan,
there at the long table.

Upcountry Carolinians
are huggers, touchers, givers,
dancers, singers, fighters, drinkers,
hunters, tellers of stories,
lovers
of God and guns,
children and country,
of women
and fierce freedom-fighting men
in time misted Scots tartans,
yesterday's gray homespun,
and today's camouflage.

Upcountry Carolinians
are people-minded,
mountain-minded.
Beloved . . .

MACARONI AND CHEESE PIE
Nancy Fletcher-Blume

I t went from snow to rain that Christmas Eve in Franklin, Tennessee, and it was almost time for the corner market on Main Street to close. The young clerks were gathered around, laughing and talking about the big Christmas party planned for the employees after closing time.

The front door opened, and gusts of cold air blew down the aisles, interrupting their carefree conversation. A woman entered the store.

She was wrapped in a heavy black coat. A big black hat was pulled low over her face, and she wore a pair of high-top, shiny yellow rain boots.

The senior stock clerk watched the woman disappear around the corner of an aisle, as the hands of the wall clock passed the closing hour. Store rules dictated that the clerks could not start checking out and securing the store until the last customer was satisfied with their shopping and on their way.

Thinking of the party, he glanced at the hands of the clock, then casually went to look for the woman, hoping maybe he could hurry her on.

He found her at the end of aisle four, between the noodles and macaroni. There she stood, in those high-top yellow boots, reading labels as though she had all the time in the world. The young clerk approached her in what he thought was a pleasant manner.

"Ma'am, can I be of some help to you?"

The woman continued reading the labels, ignoring him. As he stepped closer, he realized she was quite an old woman. The clerk knew his grandmother didn't hear well, so he thought this old woman probably couldn't hear him either.

Just as he cleared his throat and started to speak in a louder tone, she turned to him and said in a raspy voice, "Young man, have you ever had a macaroni and cheese pie?"

The question caught him off guard. "Uh . . . no, ma'am, but—"

She continued talking, not waiting for an answer. "I have probably made five hundred macaroni and cheese pies in my lifetime. Yes sir, at least five hundred of them. Forty-five years of making them." Suddenly she focused as if seeing him for the first time, dropped her head, and said, "I'm sorry. Sometimes I just plain lose track of the time."

The clerk smiled at her. "It's no bother. I'll be glad to help you find your items or check you out when you're ready."

She turned to the large metal buggy and started pushing it slowly up the long aisle, taking her time. The clerk followed. As she reached the cash register, he hurried around her and started taking the few items out.

"I have to make this macaroni and cheese pie tonight, it being Christmas Eve and all," she said. "But, you know, it seems to get larger each year."

The clerk was watching her carefully now, as he rang up the items on the counter in front of him: a huge bag of macaroni, a large block of cheese, eggs, a pound of butter, milk, and a jumbo-sized box of Ritz crackers.

"Yes, ma'am," he said, pushing the items toward the bags.

The old woman placed her big black handbag on the checkout counter and slowly opened it. Reaching down inside, she started pulling things out, one by one. Stacks of coupons secured by tight rubber bands, small packs of Kleenex, several eyeglass holders, small amber bottles of medicine, and finally, a faded red change purse.

Holding the change purse in her left hand, she carefully replaced the contents of the handbag, one by one, then attempted, with shaking fingers, to open the red change purse. Pulling a crumpled bill out, she handed it to the clerk.

He quickly counted out her change and reached to give it to her, then realized she had put the red change purse back down into the depths of the huge black one.

Seeing his hand outstretched to her, she started digging down in the black handbag again. Finding the change purse, she carefully put the few coins inside and dropped it back into the darkness of the big black bag.

The clerk was bagging the groceries, only half listening to her talk, when she leaned against the counter again, in no hurry.

"You know, years ago, I was just a young bride, and my mother-in-law taught me how to cook. She said if you bake this macaroni and cheese pie one degree over 350, it will be dry, not fit to eat."

"Yes ma'am," the clerk said, staring at her, as he shifted back and forth, holding the sack of groceries. "Can I help you out with these, ma'am?" he asked, inching toward the door.

Ignoring him, she said, "Here in Tennessee we put Ritz

crackers in our macaroni and cheese, not like they do up north. As I understand it, they just make plain macaroni and cheese."

She stared off into space with a faraway look in her eyes. "You know, I have a large family—husband, two boys, and two girls—and on every special occasion they always want me to make my macaroni and cheese pie. You know, the one with the recipe my mother-in-law gave to me."

Looking back into his eyes as though she had just remembered where she was, she continued. "You know, it was my late husband that would tease me about my forty-pound macaroni and cheese pie. I do believe it must weigh at least that when I pull it out of the oven. That recipe filled my large baking dish, and do you know, it was always eaten, down to the very last bite."

"Yes ma'am." The clerk was almost at the door now and noticed that the other two clerks had seen his dilemma and were walking over.

The old woman saw them approaching, then rambled on. "One of my girls died last year, she had the pneumonia, you know, and one of the boys lives somewhere in California. Sometimes he calls me long distance, on special occasions, and says he wishes he had some of my macaroni and cheese pie."

She paused a second, her voice dropping almost to a whisper. "The other boy moved to Colorado and is quite busy with his family, you see, and my other girl, well she lives right here in Franklin. She comes around sometimes just to check on me. Then I make the macaroni and cheese pie. But you know these fat grams the young ones talk about, well, she puts some on her plate just to be polite, and I sit, watching her just pushing it around."

By this time, all of the clerks were standing close, not knowing what to do or say to the old woman, as the clock on the wall ticked away.

"You know," she said, seeming not to be going anywhere anytime soon, "the Christmas after my husband died, I tried to make just half a recipe, but somehow it didn't taste right. I threw it out."

The older manager had walked over by this time and kindly said, "Ma'am, I'll be glad to walk you outside with your groceries, to your car, or whatever."

At this, the old woman seemed to be trying to gather her thoughts and gave the clerks standing around her a warm smile.

"I live right across the street in that apartment building," she said, "and if you'll help me now with my groceries, young man, I'll be on my way. You see, I have to hurry and make this macaroni and cheese pie for dinner tonight, it being Christmas Eve, and I mustn't be late."

Without further conversation she took her brown sack of groceries and walked out the door, not waiting for the help she had asked for.

The clerks watched her for a few seconds, shaking their heads. Then the stock clerk, remembering the party, immediately began the tasks at hand, and getting caught up in the excitement, all hurried and soon were turning the last dead bolt on the door.

Frigid winds blowing through the Tennessee hills had made the night a raw, wet one. Rain was misting the faces of the clerks as they walked through the dark parking lot. Deciding at the last minute to ride in one vehicle to the Christmas party, they crawled into the cold car.

They pulled out slowly onto the darkening street, with dimly lit streetlights starting to show, here and there.

Their low-beam headlights picked up something on the side of the road against a background of black. Shiny yellow rain boots, walking back and forth, back and forth. The boots were sloshing through the freezing mud puddles, as though they had nowhere to go and no particular time to be there.

Propped against a lamppost was a very wet sack of groceries.

AMBROSIA
Jane K. Kretschmann

One hour before time to leave
for the Christmas Eve program,
the holiday ritual begins—
grating coconut by hand,
cutting oranges with scissors
(juice running down her arms),
crushing fresh pineapple
with a short Coke bottle
saved for this annual service.
Mama refuses to hear of other
ingredients, scoffs at the suggestion
of maraschino cherries.
She pours the amber mixture
into a large old china bowl—
no Tupperware to taint the taste—
and covers it with waxed paper.
Such care you'd think she were
serving the baby Jesus Christmas
dinner, not her mere mortal in-laws.

For Jo

IT STARTED WITH A PICTURE
Marion Bolick Perutelli

World War II was in full swing in Memphis, Tennessee, where I was born and reared. I graduated high school in 1943. There were more girls than boys in that graduation class, since many of the boys had quit school to enlist in the armed services.

My father wanted to send me to college, but there were only 4F's—men turned down by the military—attending colleges. Besides, I was having too much fun to think of leaving Memphis, where I had men from all branches of the service to choose from. The Second Army was headquartered at the National Guard Armory; the Naval Air Station was at Millington, a suburb of Memphis; the Marines were stationed with the navy; and the Air Corps was at the Memphis Airport, where pilots ferried airplanes to theaters of war. I still have a collection of those ferry pilots' wings.

To add to the glamour, German prisoners were confined in Memphis at the U.S. Army Depot on Airways Boulevard. I saw them there behind high fences lined with barbed wire. Printed on their shirt backs in large black letters was PW— Prisoner of War. They were farmed out to Mississippi Delta planters to work their cotton fields.

A friend and I signed up for duty with the United

Service Organization to act as hostesses at the USO Canteen at Union Station. We handed out sandwiches, doughnuts, and coffee to servicemen. We danced and flirted with them, too. We were eighteen years old, too immature to absorb the realities of war.

Hostesses were forbidden to leave the USO Canteen with servicemen, but that didn't stop us from meeting them elsewhere. One Saturday night a naval band arrived from Millington to play for the dance at the canteen. The leader of the band told me if my friend and I would meet him on a certain corner, he would drive us home in the panel truck supplied by the navy. The band played music all the way home. Imagine my mother's surprise when I arrived at 1:00 a.m. with a naval band playing swing music.

I'd had two years of typing and shorthand in high school, so I went to work uptown as a stenographer at Aetna Casualty & Surety Company in the Goodwin Institute building, which has since been torn down. I confess I wrote personal letters from the office on Aetna's time. I wrote to servicemen from my neighborhood and to those ferry pilots who had been transferred elsewhere. I also wrote to my brother, Marshall, who joined the navy after graduating high school in 1942.

One day in the summer of 1943, I received an Air Mail, Special Delivery letter at the Aetna office from a sailor I did not know. Richard Joseph Perutelli was his name. I had to sign for his letter, so I took a chewing out from my boss, a claims attorney.

Richard had been sent from boot camp to the United States Naval Training Center at San Diego, where he met my brother. It seems that one day, Richard was standing next to my brother when Marshall opened his locker. Richard saw a picture of a girl taped to the locker door and accused Marshall of holding out on him.

"Oh, that's just my sister," Marshall said.

About that time, two other sailors came on the scene. Marshall ended up giving all three of them my work address. Richard sent his letter Air Mail, Special Delivery so it would arrive first. He warned me that I would be receiving mail from two other sailors he identified as Steve and Red. He asked me if I would write him a "mushy" letter so he could get their goats. Of course, I did. I wrote Richard two letters enclosed in same envelope. One letter was labeled "Read This First." In that letter, I complimented him on a great sense of humor and asked him to write back and describe himself. The second letter— the one he was to read to Steve and Red—I doused with perfume and called him "Richard, honey." I even put on more lipstick and pressed my lips to the back of the envelope, thereby "sealing it with a kiss." To play out the rest of the prank, I sent it Air Mail, Special Delivery. In the meantime, Steve and Red's letters arrived. I wrote to them by regular mail, which went by train. Strangely enough, I never heard from either of them again. But there were many more letters exchanged between Richard and me.

I learned from those letters that Richard was born and reared in Kansas City, Missouri. He lived just a half block off Westport Road, which was the old Santa Fe Trail leading west out of Independence, Missouri. I also learned his parents had immigrated in 1910 from Carrara, Italy. Richard measured six foot two and weighed better than two hundred pounds as a 1942 high school graduate.

He was sworn into the U.S. Navy in February, 1943. His naval buddies promptly dubbed him "Moose," a nickname he carried for the rest of his life.

After training in San Diego, Richard was assigned duty as a boilermaker second class aboard the U.S.S. North Carolina, a battleship operating in the South Pacific. He was at sea for eight months without touching land. I don't remember how many battles he participated in while aboard that ship, but he spoke often about the battle of Leyte Gulf in the Philippine Islands and of the deafening roar of the North Carolina's sixteen-inch guns.

In the summer of 1944 he was granted a thirty-day leave. After visiting his family, he flew to Memphis to see me for a week. I met him alone at the Memphis Airport, where we saw each other for the first time. I liked what I saw, and right away we clicked. He stayed at my parents' house, where I was still living. My mother had been cooking for him all morning, and he captured her heart when I introduced him. Instead of saying, "It's nice to meet you," he said, "You aren't cooking navy beans, are you?"

During that week, we became engaged. He returned to Kansas City to break the news to his parents. While en route back to San Diego, his train stopped over in Denver, where he bought a set of wedding rings, which he mailed to me after reaching the base.

Richard was assigned to a ship still under construction, the U.S.S. Coasters Harbor, and while waiting for his ship to be completed, he got another thirty-day leave. He came to Memphis, and we were married March 5, 1945, at St. Peter's Catholic Church. We were both twenty years old.

We spent our wedding night at a hotel in uptown Memphis and then took a train to Kansas City, where his parents hosted a wedding reception for us. We took separate trains out of Kansas City. We said goodbye at the train station. His train carried him back to San Diego. My train carried me back to Memphis.

After Richard got back to San Diego, he requested I send him a billfold-sized picture like the one my brother Marshall had taped to his locker door, and I did.

It was the fall of 1945 before the U.S.S. Coasters Harbor was commissioned and set out to sea, destination unknown. By that time, the war in Europe had been over several months. While Richard was at sea, the Japanese surrendered.

After the war, we went to live in Kansas City. I became homesick, so Richard brought me home to Memphis, where we moved in with my parents. He became a tool and die maker at International Harvester.

Richard bought us a half-acre lot south of the Memphis city limits in a subdivision called Prospect Park. He drew our house plans on white butcher's paper from the grocery store. It was January of 1950 before we moved into our unfinished house on Alcy Road.

Two sons came along, and the years glided by. In March of 1979, Richard and I celebrated our thirty-fourth wedding anniversary.

He loved to duck hunt, and before dawn on December 3, 1979, he and a buddy went duck hunting in Arkansas. They were setting out duck decoys in a field, which had been flooded with about two feet of water when Richard remarked, "It sure is hot, isn't it?"

Those were the last words he ever spoke. His buddy found Richard sitting in water against a tree, where a massive heart attack had felled him.

When Richard's billfold was brought to me, everything in it was wet. As I spread the contents out to dry, I found the picture of me as an eighteen-year-old. He'd carried it in his billfold for nearly thirty-five years. He'd had it laminated, so it was the only thing which wasn't water damaged.

It started with a picture. For me, it ended with that same picture.

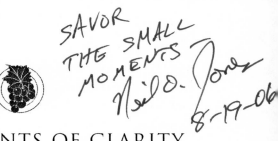

SAVOR THE SMALL MOMENTS
Neil O. Jones
8-19-06

SMALL MOMENTS OF CLARITY

Neil O. Jones

Jeanne and I were an item for six years, from the first grade through the sixth at Elisha M. Pease Elementary School in Dallas. I haven't telephoned her in, oh, about fifty years, more or less—but I still know her number. DRexel 4-3812. Our relationship was as innocent as one can be between two kids, but I bet she remembers me as a part of her growing up. I sure do remember her.

Jeanne was a small, red-haired, freckled-faced girl who was the first real brainy kid I ever knew. She could read aloud the adventures of Dick and Jane and Spot with such skill, all the classmates in Mrs. Lawhon's first grade class were impressed. Sitting three seats behind her and one row to the left, I was enthralled, listening to her read with that tiny little voice. She read with her whole body, using her face like an actress to emphasize a word. "See Spot run . . . Run Spot Run," and her head would bob and her red-orange ponytail would swing as she said it. I don't remember her ever tripping on a syllable. Lord knows, I was smitten at the age of six. Still, it took fully half of my first grade year before I had the courage to speak directly to her. And that was in the cafeteria, when I asked her if she wanted the last bite of my Spam sandwich. She just looked at me and didn't say anything, so I ate it.

Through the years in Pease Elementary, Jeanne and I were either in the same class or in classes across the hall from each other. It only took three more years for me to build up my courage, but in fourth grade I made my next move to ask her if I could walk her home. She said, "Yeah. Sure." Now I could show her what a gentleman I was, my next step at sparking Jeanne. Only later did I figure that I lived two and a half miles from school, and she lived nearly a mile on the opposite side of school. By me missing the bus and walking her home and then walking home myself, I'd have to clock in about four and a half miles. That was a lot of short, fourth-grader steps, but it was okay with me. Nobody ever said love was easy.

I was expecting to carry her books and mine, but she had a surprise for me. In art class that day she had finished a horse head she had made from paper mache. It was about three feet high to the neck, with a two-foot long head. It was black with a white blaze face and jaunty white ears. It had a big toothy grin only its creator could love. Jeanne was good at many things in school, but I could tell right off, anything in the visual arts was not her medium. She offered, but I wouldn't let her carry anything. I had two sets of books bulging off my hip on one side, and I had to kinda walk bent sideways to help support them. My other arm secured Seabiscuit by the neck.

"Are you sure you don't want me to help you?" she asked. "I could carry *something*," and she still had that cute little voice and head bob when she emphasized a word and that dandy little swing in her ponytail.

"Nah," I said. "Tain't nothing, ma'am," doing my best exaggerated cowboy drawl. She giggled and that made me feel good. "Instead of our pack mule carrying ever'thing,"

I said as I pointed to the grinning horse-thing, "I'll just carry him a spell."

The last little bit to her house was uphill, and I was huffing, but determined not to tell her that the books were feeling like rocks. "We, uh," I asked between breaths, "we getting close?"

"The house is there on the corner," she said, pointing.

We made it into her yard just as my arm was giving out and the books were slipping down my leg and into the grass. I had to make a choice on what to lose, so I held on to the black-and-white monster and let the books tumble. "I got 'em. I got 'em," I said. Gathering up the books, I placed them down easy on her front porch, right next to ol' Smiley.

"Thanks for carrying everything," she said. "You're a sweetie," and then she gave me a peck on the cheek. Four years of courtin' and two sprung arms were all worth it at that moment. "I gotta go in. I'll see you Monday," she said as she bounced off toward her side door, and her ponytail swung side to side with each stride. I walked home with my arms straight down by my side 'cause it hurt to swing them. I did hum a lot and smile some since that was the first time a girl my age had ever given me a kiss and called me "Sweetie." And I liked it.

In the fall of my sixth grade year, I got my first horse, King Royal, and he played a big part in my next event with Jeanne.

I had ridden King Royal to school a few times. Nobody said I couldn't, so I read that as I could. And maybe after seeing me ride him that far, I told myself, Jeanne would be convinced I was a safe driver, and she'd consider riding with me. The days I rode my horse to school, I kept him tied to a tree in the field across the road. At recess I'd tend to him by untangling his tether or moving him to more grass or giving him more water.

One time Jeanne asked if she could come along with me, and I said "Sure." Then I blurted out, "You wanna go to the Crest Theater Saturday morning with me? Me and King Royal here can pick you up." Only I said it so fast and mumbled my words so bad I wasn't sure she understood me. I mean I barely understood me and I knew what I was saying—sorta. I watched as her face turned nearly as red as her hair. We were beside the horse, and she started petting him on the head.

"He likes scratching right here on the neck." I showed her how with my hand over hers. King Royal leaned into the scratching. "And *The Greatest Show on Earth* is showing and it has clowns and lions and high-wire swingers and ballerinas and everything." Then I was thinking that was goofy 'cause I never saw a ballerina at a circus. Just as I was about to apologize, she disarmed me with a smile. "Sure, I'd love to go," she said, with a little laugh in her voice.

We decided I should come calling at ten Saturday morning.

It was 9:50 a.m. when King Royal turned the last corner and Jeanne's house came into view. She was sitting on the front porch—that same front porch where I had stacked books and the monster horse head years earlier. Just to show out a little, I kicked King Royal into a trot, which made him jerk his head up and look a lot more impressive than in his walk, when he held his head down low like a plow mule. She waved and I waved back and she went in the house. It was the first time I had seen Jeanne in anything but a school dress; she had on baby-blue pedal pushers with a white blouse and white canvas tennis shoes with ankle socks rolled down one time. I had no more than dismounted when she came back out accompanied by her mother. The lady was drying her hands with a dishtowel saying, "Well I'll be. I really wondered if you'd show up on a horse. Do your parents know about this?"

"Yes ma'am," I said, straight-faced as if it were true. "They're good with it. They know I'm responsible and I'll be super careful, and King Royal here, he does what I tell him to."

"Uh-huh," she said, looking at me with some doubt on her face.

"Right here behind the saddle," I said, trying to sound calm, "is where Jeanne rides. See, I put a big saddle blanket on him and got it pulled back some for a seat for her."

I didn't know what to think as her mom walked around King Royal and then stopped and petted him on the head after he raised up from tearing off a mouthful of her front yard grass. Jeanne said, "He likes petting right here," as she took her mother's hand and did some scratching on his neck. King Royal was getting a lot of good neck scratching lately.

"You know, young lady, that you will call me if there is any problem at all. You understand me?" Jeanne's mom said.

"Yes ma'am. I will," Jeanne said, beaming as she hugged her mom.

"All right then. You both have a watch, so be home right after the movie or five at the latest, and y'all go slow and be careful."

I mounted up and said, "Yes ma'am." Jeanne got up behind me with her mother's help and said, "Yes ma'am, we will."

Heading out from her house, I don't remember a more nervous time than walking King Royal down that road with Jeanne behind me. We had gone a couple of houses down when Jeanne twisted around and waved. "Bye, mom. Love you." I grabbed a quick glance back and saw her mom was smiling as she shook her head slowly back and forth. "Love you too, honey," I heard her say as she waved the dishtowel in her hand, like we were shipping out to sea or something.

As we clip-clopped along, it was kind of odd talking to Jeanne but not seeing her. I told her to hold on good because I was going to trot him and I'd let her know before I broke him into a lope. "Just go with the horse, not against him," I told her, "and you'll be fine." She learned quickly and seemed to be more relaxed as we went. She alternated between holding on to the saddle seat and my belt loops, which was sort of like holding on to me.

So far, so good. King Royal had more of a prance in his step after we picked up Jeanne. Guess he was showing off, too. My plan was to stop at Webber's Drive-In, a hamburger place on Lancaster Road, about halfway to the theater. The place had two picnic tables outside for walk up—or trot up, I guess—business. We had to duck as we rode under the carport-type cover and between two cars. To our right two kids in the back seat of a station wagon crowded to the car window and studied us silently with their mouths open. The carhop was there before we got all the way in the space.

"Well, as I live and breathe, ain't you two somethin'," she said as she laughed. Looking at me, she added, "Honey, you're gonna have to show me how to hook a tray on Trigger here."

Jeanne had a hold on my arm as I was helping her slide off. The carhop got a hold on her and said, "Let me help y'all," and she helped ease Jeanne to the ground.

I tied King Royal to the carport post and scratched him on the neck as I talked in a low tone to him. "Good job, old man. Pull this one off for me and there'll be some apples in it for you."

I turned and started to the table where Jeanne was, when I stopped and stared at her. She was always a cute girl, but this day she was the prettiest girl I had ever seen. On that bright, sunny day I noticed her shoulder length red hair had turned more blond-red over the years, and it shone as it caught the light. Her fair skin had just a tint of the sun's red, and her green eyes were bright and friendly. I thought she looked perfect. I wish I had told her so.

We talked about our order and decided we just wanted something cold to drink. Jeanne wanted a kid's mug of root beer, and I wanted a regular, adult size. I was feeling kind of big for my britches anyway. Her drink cost a nickel and mine a dime, but money was no object that day. Before I left home that morning, I had dipped into my cigar box savings.

The carhop approached and put her pencil to her order ticket and said, "What'll it be today, Roy Rogers? You and Dale ready to order?"

"Yeah," I said. "Just a small and a reg'lar root beer, please."

"We can do that," she said as she put her pencil behind her ear and her pad in her apron pocket. "They'll be right out."

The carhop brought our frosted mug root beers, and on that cooking Texas day, I had never enjoyed the taste of something more. Thin sheets of ice floated on top and slid down the sides as they warmed. I paid the carhop two dimes and told her to "Keep it." A breeze had kicked up and the shade was nice. Talking with Jeanne had never been this easy. I listened to every silly thing she had to say, and she listened to every silly thing I had to say, and the conversation was balanced and natural. The last swallow of my root beer had grown warm when I told her we had to go if we were going to get to the movie on time. I mounted King Royal and gave Jeanne a hand and a stirrup to help her up. We headed down Lancaster Road toward the Saturday matinee at the Crest.

It was five minutes before the movie started when we arrived. Some boys were standing around the bicycle stand. They stopped talking and looked, and one pointed and laughed and said something to the others and they laughed. I urged King Royal on past them and then stopped right in front of the ticket window, where I helped Jeanne slide down. I dismounted and led him around to the side of the building where there was an outside water spigot. With nothing to catch the water but my hands, I cupped them to offer King Royal a drink. He didn't understand at first so I sloshed the water up and on his mouth and nose. The next bit of water I offered him he took, as well as several more. He drank his fill and then I led him across the street to the vacant lot and tied him to a big oak tree.

As I headed for the ticket window, I noticed the inside of Jeanne's pants' legs were dark and wet from horse sweat. I apologized for it and said we didn't have to go in if she didn't want to, but she insisted she was fine and said it would dry out quickly in the air conditioned theater. I bought our tickets and gave her one and we went in and gave them to the usher. Even though the smell of popcorn was strong, I could still smell a hint of horse sweat on both of us, but I felt good and I really don't think she worried about it either.

For the twenty-five cents each I paid, we went in for a full afternoon of entertainment, including a cartoon, a newsreel, a Saturday morning serial with Lash Larue, and previews of coming attractions, all as a warm-up to the feature movie. During the newsreel I got up and went to the concession stand where I bought a box of popcorn, a large Dr. Pepper with two straws, and a box of Milk Duds. The popcorn and cold drink were a hit, but she turned down the Milk Duds, and I discovered why. When I chewed them I couldn't help but smack and they kept sticking to my teeth. Try as I might to dislodge them with my tongue, I had to probe with my finger to loosen the stuff.

About halfway through the movie, I mustered enough courage to put my arm on the top of the backrest of Jeanne's seat. Even though I tried to make it look nonchalant as I coughed a little and then swung my arm up and back, it was still awkward. I was too short and my arm was up too high. After about five minutes of my arm in the position, it started to ache, but I dared not move it 'cause it was too hard to get it up there. After another few minutes, I moved my index finger down low enough to brush the sleeve of her blouse. At least I think it was her sleeve. My arm had gone to sleep and was tingling and numb from the elbow down. Jeanne may have thought I was being forward as I rubbed back and forth with my finger on the puff of her blouse, but truthfully, with my arm asleep and all, I couldn't tell if the cloth I felt was her blouse or maybe a rip in the seat or something. I moved my eyes as far as I could toward her without moving my head to see what she was doing. She sat all prim and proper with her knees together and her ankles crossed and her hands in her lap. She was in the middle of the seat and was still as a statue with her eyes fixed on the screen. Again I got up during the movie to check on King Royal, but mainly to shake my arm back to life. He was fine, but the feeling in my arm had not fully returned when I got back to my seat. This time I sat on the other side of Jeanne. She looked surprised to see me coming from that direction, but I whispered to her that the other seat had a broke spring.

Fifteen minutes passed before I built the courage to swing my arm over again, in coordination with a phony yawn and stretch—only this time with disastrous results. When I swung my arm over, I misjudged and brought my forearm down hard in a glancing blow off her head. I heard her say "Ouch!" then "Ooooh!" I had pulled my arm back and felt the tug as I yanked her hair because my watchband had caught in it. In the confusion of trying to get untangled from one another, with her pulling and me trying to reach up and unhook us, she got her hair yanked twice more. Somehow we finally broke loose and I started apologizing. She was nice as she could be and said everything was okay. For the rest of the movie I dared no more moves. With my grace I'd more than likely have given her a black eye or a bloody nose or something. We were able to see all the movie, but we would have to head straight back to make it to her house on time. As I looked at my watch when the lights were turned up, I saw a couple of long red hairs in my watchband.

Jeanne and I talked about the movie on the way back and about other people in our class and our teachers and about things we had in common. We went from discussing the movie to talking about circus work, and Jeanne said she might be a trapeze artist someday because they were beautiful and graceful. I didn't have much to talk about when it came to being graceful, but I told her if she did decide to be a trapeze artist, she would be a good one 'cause she was pretty and graceful as a cat. Then I thought to myself that sounded dumb, but I looked back and she was smiling and I thought maybe it wasn't too dumb.

We turned into her yard eight minutes before her deadline and I was proud of that. She said she had a really nice time. I told her again I was sorry for bopping her in the head and that I sure didn't mean to yank her hair, either. She was nice again and said I should forget about it, but fifty years later, I never have.

Jeanne and I started seventh grade that next fall. Over the summer we grew apart. Other interests and other people caught our fancy.

In June of 1965, we graduated with our class at South Oak Cliff High School. The ceremony was held at Market Hall on Stemmons Freeway. Jeanne was valedictorian and gave the commencement speech. She talked about the strong bonds we all built in high school and for some of us even longer back. She said she was proud to be valedictorian, but she was more proud of the friendships she had made with the people who would be the touchstone of all future relationships. Pausing in her speech, she pushed a strand of reddish-blond hair back. "I will always remember," she continued, "the small moments of clarity that define our lives, like being with your friend and drinking a frosty root beer at Webber's Drive-In on a sweltering day. And laughing and talking so much you don't feel the heat or note the time or see anybody or anything else, and inside you are feeling near-perfect," and she looked at me as she said it, and I knew what she meant more than anyone else in that packed hall.

CONTRIBUTORS

AUTHORS

L. Ward Abel, native of Georgia, is a lifelong poet, composer of music (most recently with Abel, Rawls and Hayes), and spoken-word performer (Scapeweavel). His poems have been published worldwide, in print and online, including *White Pelican Review, The Pedestal, erbacce* (UK), *Versal* (Netherlands), *Word Riot, Texas Poetry Journal, Open Wide* (UK), *Poems Niederngasse* (Switzerland), *Southern Gothic, Dead Drunk Dublin* (Ireland), and *Tertulia.* His chapbook, *Peach Box and Verge*, was published by Little Poem Press (Falls Church, VA). His new book of poems, *Jonesing For Byzantium*, will be published late 2006 at UK Authors Press (Bristol, UK).

Mary Frazier Brennan, a native of Chattanooga, Tennessee, has spent most of her working days in Atlanta, in marketing and business communications. She has over twenty years of experience, first with Turner Broadcasting, creating short-format television scripts, and then for a high-profile architecture firm. Mary currently lives in New York City, where she works in world mission communications for The Episcopal Church.

Gilda Griffith Brown writes short fiction; her stories have appeared in online venues, including USADEEPSOUTH.COM. She has also compiled, written, and published *The Scofield Letters: Texas Pioneers*, a nonfiction work based on nineteenth-century family letters. A retired RN whose specialty was Geriatric Nursing, Gilda often finds her writing centered on the elderly—people who provide strong characters and share some of the sweetest and dearest messages of life. She lives in her hometown of Canton, Mississippi.

Chance Chambers was a top 100 winner in the Mainstream/Literary Short Story category of Writer's Digest's 73rd Annual Writing Competition for his story "Miss October." He has also been a quarter-finalist for Francis Ford Coppola's *Zoetrope: All-Story* & New Century Writers Short Story Competition, a finalist for *Glimmer Train's* Poetry Open, and a three-time nominee for the Sensored Starving Artist awards in fiction and poetry. Originally from Paris, Tennessee, Chance has lived in Nashville since 1984.

Louise Colln is the author of *San Antonio Seduction*, published by Premium Press America in April, 2006. She has written four novels for Heartsong Presents: *Birdsong Road, Falling Water Valley, Mountain House,* and *A Place for Love* (published internationally and reprinted in an anthology). Louise has adapted three children's classics for Dalmatian Press. Her Poetry in Two Voices was read at the 2005 Romanian Writers' Festival. A resident of Franklin, Tennessee, Louise is a board member of the Tennessee Writers Alliance and secretary and board member of the Williamson County Council for the Written Word.

Judy Lockhart DiGregorio was recently nominated by the Tennessee Arts Commission for inclusion in SouthernArtistry.com, an adjudicated online artist registry spotlighting outstanding Southern artists. Judy is a monthly humor columnist for *Senior Living* magazine and has published more than 100 essays, columns, and humorous poems in *The Writer, Army/Navy Times, Episcopal Life, New Millennium Writings, CC Motorcycle Newsmagazine, Church Musician Today,* and other publications. Judy is a frequent workshop presenter. She has lived in Oak Ridge, Tennessee, since 1969.

Jennifer Dix has been published in Vanderbilt Medical Center's *House Organ, Hometown* magazine, and in various other community publications. She writes poetry and creative nonfiction and is a member of the Tennessee Writers Alliance. Jennifer spent her childhood and teenage years in Weakley County, Tennessee, primarily in the small town of Palmersville. She is presently employed in market research and has worked in advertising and nonprofits. A graduate of Austin Peay State University, she currently resides in Springfield, Tennessee, with her husband and two cats.

Susie Dunham writes a column titled "All I'm Sayin' Is. . ." for *The Grassland Gazette* and *Westview* newspapers in Nashville, Tennessee, circulation 12,000. Susie, born and raised in upstate New York, is a Yankee with a Southern soul, who started taking her humor and her writing seriously at the age of 50. She has attended the Erma Bombeck Writers' Workshop and numerous other writers' conferences and is a member of the Tennessee Writers Alliance, Writers In CAPS, and the Williamson County Council for the Written Word. She currently lives in Franklin, Tennessee.

Nancy Fletcher-Blume is president of the Tennessee Writers Alliance and president of the Williamson County Council for the Written Word, as well as a ten-year founding member. She is the author of a children's book, *The Cast Iron Dogs*. She is also published in *Our Voices: Williamson County Literary Review*, 1995, 1997, and 1998. Nancy has condensed and adapted two children's classics for Dalmatian Press: Robert Louis Stevenson's *Treasure Island* (a top seller in its fourth printing) and *Kidnapped*. She signed *Treasure Island* at the 2004 Southern Festival of Books. Her poetry has received awards in several states, and her Civil War Poetry in Two Voices was read at the 2005 Romanian Writers' Festival in Bucharest. Nancy lives in Franklin, Tennessee.

Connie Foster, first grade teacher by day and writer by night, is a lifelong resident of Woodbury, Tennessee. She writes short fiction, creative nonfiction, and is completing her first novel. Connie lives with her husband, Ronnie, who struggles to communicate since a major stroke in 1997, and her son, Jake, whose ear for good storytelling supports and inspires her writing. Her story "The Sweetest Word" is a reflection of Connie's ceaseless effort to understand and empathize with those who cannot speak for themselves.

William W. (Bill) Fraker's poetry has appeared in *The Witness* magazine. He graduated from Lynchburg College with a degree in English and obtained graduate degrees from Yale University, the University of Pennsylvania, and the University of North Carolina at Chapel Hill. He has taught at Duke University and Virginia Commonwealth University. He is a psychotherapist and manager for a company improving the quality of health care in the public sector. He lives with his wife near Richmond, Virginia.

Neil O. Jones was raised in Texas, but has resided in Middle Tennessee since 1978. With a lifelong interest in writing, he has taught college English courses in Texas and Tennessee since 1974. Neil has completed a book-length collection of stories based on the quirky characters he knew and the challenges they faced in his growing-up years in the 1950s and '60s in the South Oak Cliff neighborhood of Dallas. His works have appeared in various print and online venues, including *Perceptions 2005, 2006; Southern Humorists.com*; and *Southern Hum*. Neil and his wife reside in the country near Columbia, Tennessee, with their hounds and horses.

Jane K. Kretschmann's works have appeared or are forthcoming in *ByLine, Waterways: Poetry in the Mainstream, Writer's Journal, Fresh Boiled Peanuts, Artistry of Life, Right Hand Pointing, Wavelength: Poetry in Prose and Verse, Common Threads, Sandcutters, Ohio Poetry Day Best of 2003 and 2004, NFSPS Encore 2005, The Farmer's Daughter* anthology, the NPR program "Theme and Variations," the Dayton Metro Library Web site, and the Akron (Ohio) Art Museum Web site, on which her poem "Crazy Quilt" was posted. Jane grew up in Alabama and lives in Ohio, where she is an Associate Professor of English and a member of the Edison Writers' Club.

Joyce A. O. Lee is the author of the novel *The Length of a Love Song*, published in 2005 by Cold Tree Press. Her poems were included in *Our Voices: Williamson County*

Literary Review, 1997 and 1998. She attended Columbia State Community College, where she studied literature, English composition, and creative writing. She has studied creative writing with Richard Speight; Clay Stafford; Darnell Arnoult; and Maggie Vaughn, Poet Laureate of Tennessee. She is a member of the Tennessee Writers Alliance and the Williamson County Council for the Written Word. Joyce is originally from Kansas City, Missouri, and has lived in the Middle Tennessee area since 1973. She has been writing full time for fifteen years.

S. R. Lee is the author of *Granny Lindy*, published in 2005. She writes fiction, short nonfiction, and poetry. Sally has a Christmas carol published by Oxford University Press. She took the Woodland Award for Best Poet in the Cookeville Creative Writers' Contest, May 2000, and has read at the Southern Festival of Books in Nashville. She was contributing editor of *The Poets of St. Paul's*, an anthology of St. Paul's Episcopal Church, Franklin, Tennessee. She has also worked on extensive "family lore" documents for other people and is currently preparing an anthology of historical articles on Beechville, the former name of the community in which she lives. Sally has spent her lifetime in Middle Tennessee. She and her husband live on the family farm, where their daughter trains horses.

Ginger Manley is a seventh-generation Tennessean, who resides with her husband in Williamson County. After forty years in health care, the last twenty-five of which she specialized as a Certified Sex Therapist, Ginger has recently closed her professional practice to pursue a new career as a writer. Her four grandchildren provide rich experiences for her personal essays, and her years of clinical practice and life in general are nourishing the background for a fictional trilogy Ginger is writing about sex, God, and dancing, and the redemption of three southern women.

Ben Norwood is the author of *Plenum*, a collection of poems, published by SRLR Press of Austin, Texas. Seventy-four of his poems, stories, and translations have been published since 1973 in journals and magazines throughout the USA. Ben attended the University of Texas at Austin and Southern Methodist University. He was a Gulbenkian Foundation fellow at the University of Lisbon in 1973. He has been a member of The Writer's Garret, the Tennessee Writers Alliance, the Association of Literary Translators, and the Academy of American Poets. He is a native of Dallas, Texas, and currently resides in Franklin, Tennessee.

Lonnye Sue Sims Pearson is Associate Editor and Message Board Manager for USADEEPSOUTH.COM—*"Best Spot for all Things Southern!"*—where many of her favorite memoirs are published, including her story "Mamaw and the Night Visitor." She has also been published in the e-zine *Queen Power* and in *Tombigbee Country Magazine*. Lonnye Sue is an eighth grade English teacher, who writes memoirs in her spare time and maintains an online journal for sanity's sake. She is a Mississippi Delta native, who now resides in Kinston, North Carolina.

Marion Bolick Perutelli is a native Tennessean, reared in Memphis. She is the author of a historical novel, *The Mud Daubers*, and a novella, *From Whence He Came And Short Stories*, both set in Memphis and published by Cold

Tree Press in 2005. Her short stories and essays have been published in newspapers and anthologies, including *Our Voices: Williamson County Literary Review*, 1995, 1997, and 1998. Marion was a charter member of the Tennessee Writers Alliance. Currently a resident of Brentwood, Tennessee, she is also a member of WordSmiths, Ink; the Council for the Written Word; and the Fiction Writers at The Martin Center of Senior Citizens.

Julia Lee Pollock (Gillen) writes "Random Lives," a bi-monthly column, as well as feature stories for *The Daily Herald* in Columbia, Tennessee. She serves on the Editorial Committee of the Maury County Archives, and she is a member of ASCAP. She has completed her first novel, *A Southern Dog's Tale*. Julia lives in Columbia, Tennessee.

Currie Alexander Powers is the author of the novel *Soul of a Man*, published by Cold Tree Press. Her writing has also appeared in *Tin House*. Though she was born in Toronto, Canada, her heart belongs to the bayous of Louisiana and the Mississippi Delta. Currie spent her early years working as a musician, playing and recording with such artists as The CeeDees, Bruce Cockburn, Rick Danko and Stephen Fearing. She is also a songwriter, and her songs have been recorded by Sara Craig and Blackie & The Rodeo Kings, among others. She lives in Nashville, Tennessee, with her husband and four cats.

Nelda Rachels is a freelance writer who has published poetry and nonfiction in *Purdue's Writing Lab Newsletter, The Draft Horse Journal, Country Handcrafts, Back Home in Kentucky, Hometown,* and others. She enjoys her part-time job tutoring writers and students in the Hortense Parrish Writing Lab at the University of Tennessee at Martin. She has been married to her master gardener husband for thirty-three years and has two grown children. In her spare time, she loves to read nonfiction on her front porch.

Thomas D. Reynolds teaches at Johnson County Community College in Overland Park, Kansas, and has published poems in various print and online journals, including *New Delta Review, Alabama Literary Review, Aethlon-The Journal of Sport Literature, The MacGuffin, Flint Hills Review, Midwest Poetry Review, Potpourri, Ariga, Strange Horizons, Combat, American Western Magazine, The Pedestal Magazine, Ash Canyon Review,* and *Orphan Leaf Review.*

C. K. Speroff is a writer of stories drawn from the heartache and joy of being female—a daughter, a wife, a mother. Born in Arkansas and raised in Oklahoma, she now resides in Franklin, Tennessee. Writer of fiction and nonfiction, C. K. is a member of Writers in CAPS and the Williamson County Council for the Written Word.

Linda Therber has published in community and educational newsletters, a parents' magazine, the "Nashville Eye" op-ed column of *The* (Nashville) *Tennessean*, and as a contributor in a book on multicultural teaching strategies. Born in Montgomery, Alabama, she grew up in Middle Tennessee, where she currently resides. Her writing is rooted in family stories and oral histories that are culled for unspoken words, unguarded moments, and simple truths.

Kristin O'Donnell Tubb writes both fiction and nonfiction for children and adults. A recipient of the Pewter Plate Award for Best Arts Feature in 2005 from *Highlights for Children* magazine, Kristin has also published stories in *Cricket, Spider, Guideposts for Kids,* and *Wee Ones eMagazine.* She has written a number of children's activity books, many for licensed characters such as Holly Hobbie™, The Powerpuff Girls™, Scooby-Doo™, Strawberry Shortcake™, and the Care Bears™. She is the author of a high-school-targeted anthology, *Freedom from Cruel and Unusual Punishment,* published by Greenhaven Press in 2005. Kristin has also published travel articles in *The* (Nashville) *Tennessean* and *Woodall's Regionals,* and leisure pieces in *Collector's News* and *Antiques and Collecting Magazine.*

Kathleen Vibbert's works have been published in *Spillway Review, Electric Acorn, Facets: A Literary Magazine, Lily: A Literary Review, The Criterion Newspaper, Softblow Poetry Journal, Moondance,* and *Celebrating Creative Women.* She enjoys scrapbooking and studying creative writing. Currently, she lives with her husband in Indiana and has three adult children. Her daughter is a graduate of Ole Miss, and Kathleen was greatly inspired by the South during her daughter's stay in Oxford, Mississippi.

Kory Wells' novel-in-progress *White Line to Graceville* was a finalist in the William Faulkner Competition. A software developer, she writes about her desire to be an astronaut and living beyond traditional cultural roles in the anthology *She's Such a Geek* (Seal Press, 2006). Her prose has appeared or is forthcoming in various venues, including *Birmingham Arts Journal, Long Story Short,* and *The Cuivre River Anthology,* in which her story "Trade Day" first appeared. A native Tennessean who has frequented flea markets and antique malls since she was a child, Kory is able to park in her garage but confesses that her bonus room is virtually impassable.

EDITOR

Kathy Hardy Rhodes is Editor of the online magazine *Muscadine Lines: A Southern Journal* and the author of *Pink Butterbeans: Stories from the heart of a Southern woman,* a collection of fifty personal essays. Her works have appeared in magazines, newspapers, and literary anthologies, including *Our Voices: Williamson County Literary Review,* 1995, 1997, and 1998, and Simon & Schuster's nationally distributed *Chocolate for a Woman's Soul II.* Born and raised in the Mississippi Delta, she currently resides in Franklin, Tennessee, where she is a member of the Tennessee Writers Alliance and treasurer of the Williamson County Council for the Written Word.

Printed in the United States
55542LVS00002B/52-90